Mary Boyle

Biographical catalogue of the portraits at Weston, the seat of the Earl of Bradford

Mary Boyle

Biographical catalogue of the portraits at Weston, the seat of the Earl of Bradford

ISBN/EAN: 9783741198816

Manufactured in Europe, USA, Canada, Australia, Japa

Cover: Foto ©Andreas Hilbeck / pixelio.de

Manufactured and distributed by brebook publishing software (www.brebook.com)

Mary Boyle

Biographical catalogue of the portraits at Weston, the seat of the Earl of Bradford

BIOGRAPHICAL CATALOGUE.

BIOGRAPHICAL CATALOGUE

OF THE PORTRAITS

AT WESTON

THE SEAT OF THE

EARL OF BRADFORD

'A true delineation, even of the smallest man, and his scene of pilgrimage through life, is capable of interesting the greatest man; for all men are to an unspeakable degree brothers, each man's life a strange emblem of every man's, and human portraits faithfully drawn are, of all pictures, the welcomest on human walls.'
— CARLYLE.

LONDON: ELLIOT STOCK

1888.

TO

LORD AND LADY BRADFORD,

THESE PAGES,

WRITTEN UNDER THE PRESSURE OF MANY DIFFICULTIES,

ARE AFFECTIONATELY INSCRIBED

BY THEIR FAITHFUL KINSWOMAN

MARY BOYLE.

IN completing the last contribution I shall make to the Biographical Catalogues of the Portrait Galleries of four English noblemen, I must make a few personal remarks. I began the pleasant task, which I undertook at the request of my dear cousin, Lord Sandwich, now many years ago, before my defective sight rendered the work difficult. The respective collections of Lords Bath and Cowper at Longleat and Panshanger next occupied my attention, but the increasing malady in my eyesight rendered every fresh step more arduous. In this last work, to other stumbling-blocks has been added the pressure of ill-health and deep sorrow; against these obstacles I have fought as stoutly as I could, cheered on by the hope of giving satisfaction to Lord and Lady Bradford, to whose family my own for many generations has been connected by ties of relationship and friendship. But I am well aware that in spite of my best endeavours errors may have crept into this work, and shortcomings must be but too evident. On the indulgence of the owners of Weston, I must, therefore, rely for pardon; proffering at the same time my best thanks to Lord Bradford himself for the kind help he has afforded me; while to Mr. George Griffiths of Weston Bank I can scarcely say enough to express my gratitude for his unwearied and valuable assistance. I wish that, in relinquishing a task in which I have found great delight, I could persuade some members of noble and gentle families to follow my example in rescuing from oblivion the records of portraits which adorn the walls of their homes. It has often been a subject of deep concern to me, while staying in some beautiful country-house, to find that the younger portion of the family, at least, were often entirely ignorant of any details respecting the lives of the men and women who look down upon them from the walls, and who in some cases have lived, loved, enjoyed, suffered, and died in those very apartments. To the dear old traditions of home such acquaintance with our predecessors and their surroundings lends many a charm, and I have found so much pleasure in my work that I cannot but regret my inability to the further prosecution thereof; but I have reaped a rich reward in the acquaintance I have made with particulars of the lives of the great, the good, and the celebrated; and as

I wander through a portrait-gallery, the paintings of which are, alas! now but a closed book to me, the names which my more fortunate companions read aloud conjure up a whole host of delightful and interesting recollections.

22 SOUTH AUDLEY STREET,
August 9th, 1888.

ENTRANCE HALL.

A

ENTRANCE HALL.

No. 1. RACHEL, LADY RUSSELL.

In widow's weeds. Leaning her cheek on her hand.

BORN (*circa*) 1636, DIED 1723.

BY VANDERBANK.

HE was the second daughter of Thomas, last Earl of Southampton, of the Wriothesley family, by his first wife, Rachel de Ruvigny, of an old Huguenot race, by whom he had two daughters, Elizabeth married to Edward, Lord Noel, eldest son of the Earl Campden, and Rachel, the subject of the present notice. She lost her mother when still a little child, and we do not hear much of her youth. Her father married a second and a third time, and it must have been about 1653 that she became the bride of Lord Vaughan, son of the Earl of Carbery. We are inclined to deduce from a passage in one of her letters that this marriage was one of *convenance*, as she says to a friend, 'The selection of the partners usually rests with the relations, and not with those most interested in the matter.' Of Lord Vaughan we have few records; but some letters addressed to his wife leave the impression that indolence was one of his chief characteristics, that he was

dilatory in business and averse to writing of all kinds. It is fair, however, to add that these remarks are only based on surmise.

Lord and Lady Vaughan resided chiefly at an estate in Wales, belonging to Lord Carbery, and at the present time (1888) the property of the Earl of Cawdor. The Golden Grove is famed for its picturesque beauty, and endeared to all admirers of Jeremy Taylor, by the tradition that he composed *The Whole Duty of Man* in the grounds adjoining the house. Lord and Lady Vaughan made occasional visits to London, where in 1665 she gave birth to a daughter, who only lived a few days. The breaking out of the plague drove them back to their Welsh home, and Lord Vaughan died not long after their return. On becoming a widow, Rachel went to reside for some time with her sister, Lady Elizabeth Noel, at their old home of Titchfield, in Hampshire, which had come by inheritance to Lady Elizabeth, as the eldest daughter of Lord Southampton,—Stratton, in the same county, falling to Lady Vaughan's share. It was not long before (among many admirers) that William Russell, the second son of Francis, fifth Earl (afterwards first Duke) of Bedford, made himself conspicuous by the devoted court he paid to the beautiful young widow. The circumstance is thus alluded to, in a letter from her sister by half-blood, Lady Percy : ' For Mr. Russell's concern I can say nothing more than that he professes a great desire (the which I do not at all doubt) that he and every one else has to gain one who is so desirable in all respects.'

Desirable indeed, for Lady Vaughan was young, beautiful, intellectual, wealthy, of a most gentle and loving disposition, and possessing a fund of unassuming piety. There was no disparity in the marriage, for William Russell was her equal, we might almost say her counterpart, with the exception of fortune, he being a second son at the time of his marriage.

It was on this account that his wife for some time, in fact until the death of her brother-in-law, Lord Russell, still retained, according to general custom, her widowed title of Lady Vaughan. During the fourteen happy years of Rachel's happy life, which were chiefly spent at Stratton, and Southampton House in London (both of which were hers by inheritance), she had to endure very few separations from her husband—such as when he was called away on public or private business; occasional visits to his father at Woburn; absences contingent on his elections in three different Parliaments, and attendance during the short session at Oxford. Then the correspondence between the married pair was constant and detailed, and testifies to their sympathy on every subject, whether important or trifling, political or domestic. Happy as she was in the present, with every human probability of the continuance of that happiness in the future, there was a strange foreboding, as it would appear, in Rachel's mind, of coming evil, and it was remarkable how in those early halcyon days her mental eyes seemed fixed on the little cloud, no bigger than a man's hand, in the horizon. It was indeed as if she heard 'the footfall of fate on her ear'; for her letters to her husband, not very long after their marriage, are written in a most desponding spirit. After dwelling with gratitude and delight on the complete unity of their hearts and minds, she goes on to write to her dearest William, dated from Stratton: 'Let us cheerfully expect to live together to a good old age, and, if God wills otherwise, then firmly believe that He will support us under whatsoever trial He may see fit to inflict.' Noble and pathetic words, of which the sadder alternative was to be her allotted portion. The summer was usually passed at Stratton, the winter in London. Three children were born to them—two daughters, in 1674 and 1676, and a son in 1680,—blessings which were counterbalanced by the loss of her beloved sister, Lady Elizabeth

Noel. The society of the children enhanced the delight of their beloved home at Stratton. On one occasion Rachel wrote to her husband at the last-mentioned place from Southampton House in answer to a letter from him. She is so glad he finds Stratton sweet, and hopes he will live for fifty years to enjoy it, and that God may permit her to have his good company. But if it were not so, she is sure he would be kind to 'the brats.' Flesh and blood cannot have a truer sense of happiness than she has, his poor honest wife. Such simple extracts are truly pathetic, when we call to mind that in less than two years Rachel Russell was a widow. The circumstances of Lord Russell's arrest, his impeachment for high treason, his trial, sentence, last days, and execution, with the part his devoted wife took in all these proceedings, are all given in our notice of Lord Russell's life. In order to avoid repetition we simply give the dates here. William, Lord Russell, was tried on the 13th of July 1683, and executed the 21st August.

After the last sad scene of leave-taking, elsewhere described, Rachel returned to her desolate home of Southampton House. On the anguish of such moments it is useless to dwell. She heard the hours from the neighbouring belfry, which sounded like a chime of knells, as she sat in perfect solitude—the little ones having cried themselves to sleep. Her favourite sister, Elizabeth, was dead ; her surviving sister, Lady Northumberland, was out of England, and there was no one near enough her heart whose society she could tolerate at that supreme moment. Her grief was embittered and her indignation roused, not long after her lord's death, by the report that was circulated calling in question the authenticity of the papers which he had given to the sheriffs on the scaffold. She found it incumbent on her to write to the King, speaking in the highest terms in her letter of Bishop Burnet, who had lately fallen into disfavour at Court. Burnet had been privy to the document written by Lord Russell in prison, and Rachel characterises the prelate as a loyal subject to the King, and the most tender and faithful minister to her dear lord. One of the last injunctions laid upon her (by one whose wishes were never disobeyed), was that she should take care of her health, and live for her children; and in the fulfilment of that duty she found her best consolation. In a letter to the Bishop of London, she says that she considered there was something so sublime in the subject of her deepest sorrow, she firmly believes it had in a degree kept her from being overwhelmed. And now began the long dreary period of widowhood which lasted so many years. 'Time, that ancient nurse,' which 'rocks us to patience,' found her indeed submissive, but had little power to deaden the poignancy of her grief. In a letter to 'uncle John' (her lord's uncle), she begs him to make some compliment of her acknowledgment to his Majesty for not having enforced the forfeiture of Lord Russell's fortune. She concludes by saying: 'When I hear you are well it is part of the only satisfaction I can have in this wretched world, where the love and company of the friends and relations of that dear blessed person are most precious.'

Among Lady Russell's most frequent and most intimate correspondents was Dr. Fitzwilliam, the friend of her childhood, who had been her father's domestic chaplain. She also continued her intercourse with Bishop Burnet, and tells him how diligently she superintends the education of her children, Mistress Rachel, little Mistress Katey, and that precious boy with whose wild freaks in happier days she was wont to entertain papa. She confesses to the Bishop that she occasionally finds the employment of teaching irksome to her overtaxed spirit; yet on the whole it refreshes her, and she is resolved to prosecute the task alone and unassisted. This plan the Bishop highly approves, and he alludes to the circumstance in these words : ' I am glad your children will need no other governess, for as it is the greatest part of your duty, so the occupation will be a noble entertainment, and the best diversion and cure for your wasted and wearied spirit.' It is to Bishop Burnet that she describes her sensations on visiting her husband's tomb at Chenies : ' I did not go to seek the living among the dead, for I well knew that I should see him no more, wherever I went, and I had made a covenant with myself not to break out into unreasonable and fruitless passion, but quicken my contemplation of his happiness.'

There are two classes of mourners most prevalent in the world, those who give way to enervating emotion, nursing and encouraging the outward expression of grief, and those who fly to some frivolous and unworthy expedient to ' lull the lone heart and banish care.' To neither of these classes did Lady Russell belong; she faced her affliction bravely but submissively, believing with the poet [1] that

'They who lack time to mourn, lack time to mend.
Eternity mourns that.'

She spent a great deal of her time at Woburn, with her parents-in-law, where she and her children were ever welcome; often meditating, and frequently delaying her return to the once happy home of sweet Stratton. But she was detained at Woburn first by the death of her mother-in-law, and then by the dangerous illness of her son, which crushing anxiety she thus turns to good account. Speaking of the possibility of losing 'the little creature,' she writes to Dr. Fitzwilliam, ' God has made me see the folly of imagining I had nothing left, the deprivation of which could be matter of much anguish, or its possession of any considerable refreshment.' But the blow was averted and the boy recovered. She left Woburn, and instead of going direct to Stratton she started for Totteridge

[1] Philip van Artevelde.

in Hertfordshire, with him and her eldest girl, while little Katey was left at Woburn to keep company with her aged grandfather.

No one was more alive to the noble and loveable qualities of Lady Russell than her dear lord's father, and he writes her a most tender and pathetic letter, evincing the deepest interest in her and her children, especially in the recovery of the young heir, whose illness had caused so much anxiety to the whole family. He addresses her as his dearest daughter, and expresses himself in the quaint and courteous, though somewhat stilted style of the day, hoping soon to have some comfortable tidings of her and her dear little ones, assuring her that his grandson is the subject of his constant prayers, and that while he has breath he remains her affectionate father and friend to command. Written from Woburn Abbey, the 7th day of June 1684; with a postscript: 'My dear love and blessing to my dear boy, and to Mistress Rachel. I am much cheered by Mistress Catherine's company; she is often with me, and looks very well.' It is interesting to remember that the respective ages of these two playfellows were nine, and eighty.

Lady Russell moved afterwards with her family to Southampton House, so full of memories, sweet and bitter, of early happiness, subsequent anxiety, and utter desolation. She was in London at the time of the King's death, and although she had no reason to regret Charles, yet to one whose interest was never deadened in the course of public affairs, there was little to be hoped for in the accession of James the Second. The trials of Algernon Sidney, Hampden, and others, who were associated with the memory of her lord, made her wounds bleed afresh, more especially the execution of the Duke of Monmouth, Lord Russell's most intimate friend. 'Never,' she writes, 'had a poor creature more *awakers* to quicken and revive her sorrow'; yet in alluding to Monmouth's fate she owns herself void of reason, that she should weep when she ought to rejoice 'that so good a man is safely landed on the blessed shores of a safe eternity.' She was detained in London longer than she wished by the arrival of her uncle the Marquis de Ruvigny, who had come over from France to assist in the endeavour to gain from the King and Government the subversion of the attainder which affected the Russell children. Very interesting letters and documents on this subject are extant at Woburn Abbey. Lady Russell was very much attached to her uncle, and welcomed him, his wife, and a favourite niece, to her house, where the last-mentioned relative fell sick of malignant fever and died, to the inexpressible grief of De Ruvigny. Rachel's anxiety on account of her own children may be imagined; she removed them to the country, and then returned to London to comfort her sorrowing uncle. De Ruvigny later on resided permanently in England, and became the centre of a small colony of French refugees which settled at Greenwich, and he ended his days in this country. The Earl of Devonshire, the faithful friend (when Lord Cavendish) of William Russell, who had offered to change clothes with him and remain in his stead in prison, had never slackened in his friendship for his friend's widow; and he now came forward with a proposal of marriage between his eldest son and Rachel's eldest daughter and namesake.

In those days no time was lost in such matters. My Lord Cavendish was sixteen, Mistress Rachel fourteen. There were difficulties about settlements (*car l'histoire se répète*) among the lawyers, but the marriage did come off at last in spite of those everlasting impediments to the course of true love. Deeply interested as she was in domestic details and in arrangements for the future of her child, Lady Russell was no indifferent spectator to the rapid strides which James the Second was making towards the downfall of political and religious liberty which he was too short-sighted to foresee would include his own. When M. Dykeveldt, the minister plenipotentiary from Holland, arrived in London, he waited on Lady Russell by the commands of the Prince and Princess of Orange, being the bearer of autograph letters and the most flattering messages from their Highnesses, speaking in terms of the highest admiration and esteem of her patriot lord and the noble family to which he belonged, and assuring her of friendship and sympathy and the hope that they might in the future be useful to her and her son. Thus commenced a correspondence which brought forth important fruits in the coming changes. Her first visit to Stratton was very trying to her heart, and though grateful that the children were too young to share those feelings to any great extent, she could not but rejoice to perceive in Mistress Rachel some memory of the loss they had sustained, but then to be sure, as the reader will take into consideration, Rachel Russell the younger was already fourteen years of age and a promised wife! Three days the poor widow always gave to seclusion and reflection, the anniversaries of the arrest, trial, and execution of her lord. In the winter the family removed to London, and preparations were now going on briskly for the marriage, when the poor *fiancée* fell sick of the measles, and it was not till midsummer 1689 that the celebration of the marriage actually took place, being hurried at the last, we are told, because my Lord (Devonshire, the bridegroom's father) was in haste to go to the Bath.

The young couple spent their (crescent) honeymoon between Southampton House and Woburn Abbey, and then the bridegroom set forth on a course of foreign travel to finish his education which lasted two years, while my Lady Cavendish remained an inmate of her mother's home. The leading members of the houses of Cavendish and Russell were among those influential personages who had invited the Prince and Princess of Orange to come over to England to the rescue of the kingdom; and when they actually landed Rachel put herself in constant communication with her old friend Bishop Burnet, at that time in the suite of the future monarchs. She accompanied her aged father-in-law to London, in time to witness the flight of James the Second, and there is extant an amusing letter from young Lady Cavendish in which she describes to a bosom friend, the decision of the two Houses of Parliament that William and Mary of Orange should be King and Queen. She goes on to say she was present at the proclamation, which gave her great pleasure, 'for were they not in the room of King James, my father's murderer?' At night she went to Court to kiss the Queen's hand, the King's also, with her mother-in-law, the Countess of Devonshire. She describes William 'as a man of no presence; he is homely at first sight, but when one looks long on him he has something both wise and good.' The Queen she considers very handsome, and most graceful.

One of the first acts of the new King and Queen was the reversal of the attainder of William, Lord Russell; his execution had already been declared to be a murder by the vote of the House of Commons. Honours of different kinds were showered on the aged Earl of Bedford, the Earl of Devonshire, and many of Lady Russell's connections and friends, while she herself was constantly referred to for advice and counsel by people whom she held in great esteem, such as Dr. Fitzwilliam and Archbishop Tillotson, who discussed with her questions of doctrine and faith, and the propriety or expediency of accepting preferment under the new *régime*. People of all opinions applied to Rachel to secure her good offices with the new Sovereigns, and Lady Sunderland, whose husband had been most instrumental in Lord Russell's downfall, did not scruple to ask her intercession. Passing years brought fresh trials in their train for one who seemed indeed born for sorrow. In 1690 she lost her remaining sister, the wife of Ralph, Lord afterwards Duke of Montagu, and within a few weeks of her death she mourns that of her nephew Lord Gainsborough, 'that engaging creature,' she writes, 'the only son of the sister whom I loved with so much passion,' and now as a crowning grief she is threatened with blindness. It had been said that this infirmity proceeded from her constant weeping; and though one of her biographers argues that it was impossible on account of the particular nature of the disease, being cataract, those who unfortunately have experience in such cases know well how noxious to the sight is the briny nature of sorrow's flood. It is piteous to read her sad anticipations of the coming evil, and how she will have to forego that great relaxation and comfort to her, of what she terms 'society at a distance. But while light is left her she will work.'

Lord Cavendish having now returned from the Continent was joined by his young wife, and there was a sad gap when dearest Rachel left her home. The fond mother writes to Lady Derby, Mistress of the Robes to Queen Mary, recommending her daughter, who was much at Court, to that lady's kind protection; and now yet another of the young birds was called on to leave the nest. Mistress Kate was asked in marriage by Lord Roos, eldest son of the Earl of Rutland, esteemed the best match in all England. Yet there were reasons of a political and domestic nature which caused Lady Russell to hesitate before giving her final consent to the marriage. There is an amusing description of the grand reception which the newly married pair met with at the paternal estate of Belvoir, falling very little short of the pomp and splendour due to royalty on such occasions. We regret that our want of space precludes the introduction of some interesting details. Rachel did not go to the marriage, for noise and too much company made her eyes ache, and she was desirous to keep 'the little bit of sight she had left,' which deserted her as soon as a candle was lighted. There was still balm in Gilead. The operation for couching was successfully performed, and the patient, after making use of an amanuensis for some time, was able once more to resume her correspondence and enjoy 'society at a distance.' Following this inestimable blessing came the mark of royal favour which must have been a source of intense gratification to Rachel, Lady Russell. Her son-in-law and her father-in-law were both advanced to the rank of Dukes of Devonshire and Bedford. And in the case of the latter, the honour was enhanced to the old man, Lady Russell, and the whole family, by the tribute paid in the words of the patent to the memory of his patriot son. Sure never was sentiment so mingled before or since with legal and formal documents, but the words (or preamble as it is called) were those of the eloquent and refined Lord Chancellor Somers. The King in bestowing the highest dignity in his gift declares, 'We think it not sufficient that his (Lord Russell's) conduct and virtues should be transmitted to all future generations upon the credit of public annals, but will have them inserted in these our royal letters-patent as a monument consecrated to the most accomplished and consummate virtue,' etc. etc. All honour to the house whose patent of nobility well deserves the name!

A general election was now impending, and Lady Russell received the most flattering proposals from the leading members of the Government, that her son should represent Middlesex in the House of Commons. She makes a very gracious answer, and after taking counsel with the aged Duke, she writes they have both come to the conclusion that a Parliament life would interfere with the progress of Lord Tavistock's education, he being only fifteen. Strange times when schoolboys married and sat in Parliament! The young heir went to Oxford (instead of to the House), where he was more than once visited by his mother.

When about seventeen Lord Tavistock started with a private tutor on a continental tour, which lasted over two years, and which the young man enjoyed perhaps a little too much. He made his mother a confidante of all his pleasures, extravagancies, and escapades, for Tavistock was one of those who loved the beautiful, whether in sights, sounds, or people. He had also grand notions of the style in which the heir to an English dukedom should live—must have a carriage with a fine pair of steppers and two running footmen; his cravats must be of rich point lace, and his suits finely embroidered. Moreover he found himself constrained to send all the way from Rome to Leghorn to procure a periwig, as the world's capital could not furnish him with one to his taste. Then there were flowers and gifts of jewels to please the fair Romans, and added to all these ways and means of getting rid of his pocket-money, our traveller had a decided inclination for gambling. His letters are the natural outpourings of an enthusiastic youth in the heyday of spirits and enjoyment, rather too easily led astray, and although they caused his mother some distress, they contained nothing likely to diminish her esteem for her only son. He confessed his delinquencies so frankly, solicited help so humbly, and begged his beloved mother's pardon, and her intercession for that of his grandfather, in a most irresistible manner.

Within a year after Lord Tavistock's return to England, he succeeded to his grandfather's titles and estates on the death of that good old man, and in compliance with personal request made by his mother, the King bestowed on him the Garter, and shortly afterwards he was appointed Lord-Lieutenant of the three counties of Bedford, Middlesex, and Cambridge, while at the Coronation of Queen Anne he acted as Lord High Constable of England, and was made a Privy Councillor. He had married in 1669 the daughter of John Howland, Esquire, who was created Lord Howland of Streatham, in order to obviate any appearance of a *mésalliance.* But all this prosperity was of short duration; eleven years after his accession to the title, at the early age of thirty-one, Wriothesley, the second Duke of Bedford, fell a victim to the terrible disease, which in those days (before inoculation or vaccination was known) wrought such ravages in England. When the character of the illness was announced, the Duchess and his children were sent to a distance, but the fond mother watched by his bedside to the last, and writes, after all is over, to her cousin Lord Galway: 'I am in such disorder of spirits, so full of confusion, and amazement, that I am incapable of saying or doing what I should. I did not know the greatness of my love for his person, till I could see it no more.' The poor mourner had scarcely time to lift her head, bowed by the combined weight of age and sorrow, before another crushing blow fell on her. Her sweet Katey (now Duchess of Rutland) died in giving birth to her tenth child, at the same moment that the Duchess of Devonshire was expecting her confinement. From her Lady Russell had the arduous task of concealing the fact of the other's death. The two sisters had loved each other tenderly, and there was great difficulty in evading the inquiries which the Duchess constantly made after her dear Katey. 'I saw her yesterday,' was the sad subterfuge, 'out of her bed.' Alas! it was in her coffin.

The Duke of Rutland was not slow in providing himself with a second wife, and this unseemly haste was not calculated to soothe Lady Russell's mind, but when she found that his intentions with regard to her daughter's children were just and generous, she thought it advisable 'to let the matter pass easily.' She had now arrived at an advanced age, somewhat infirm in body, but unimpaired in mind, with a trembling hand, but an unclouded intellect, and she busied herself in composing prayers and meditations for her own use, and in making, as it were, a full confession of her failings and shortcomings (which she called sins); reviewing as she did so the whole of her past life. This document was left unfinished at the time of her death. When at the age of eighty-six, her health gave way.

A letter from Lady Rachel Morgan (wife of Sir William Morgan of Tredegar) to her brother, Lord James Cavendish, says : 'The bad account we have received of Grandmamma Russell has put us into great disorder and hurry. Mamma has left us and gone to London. I believe she has stopped the letters, so we are still in suspense ; the last post brought us so bad an account that we have reason to fear the worst. I hope mamma will get to town in time to see her alive, because it would be a great satisfaction to both.' This letter is dated 26th September. On the 29th of the same month 1723, Rachel, Lady Russell, ended her exemplary and blameless life, so replete with stirring incidents, both of a public and private nature, so full of transient joy and abiding sorrow. She lived to see her children raised to honour and prosperity, but, alas! she had the misfortune to survive those who, in the common course of nature, should have wept her loss. She was buried by the side of her dear lord at Chenies, in Buckinghamshire, where an elaborate monument is erected to their memory.

No. 2.   LADY ROBERT RUSSELL.

Oval. Tawny and blue dress.

BY SIR GODFREY KNELLER.

SHE was the daughter of Edward Russell, and widow of Thomas Cheek of Pirgo, county Sussex. She married her cousin, Lord Robert Russell.

No. 3. SIR ORLANDO BRIDGEMAN, LORD CHIEF JUSTICE.

In robes of office: scarlet and ermine, with cap and gold chain. Gloves in left hand.

BORN 1609.   DIED 1674.

BY RILEY.

No. 4. LORD ROBERT RUSSELL.

Oval. Dark brown dress.   Wig.   Lace cravat.

DIED 1722.

BY SIR GODFREY KNELLER.

E was the fifth son of the first Duke of Bedford, by Anne Carr, daughter of the Earl of Somerset. He married his cousin in 1690, the widow of Thomas Cheek, by whom he had no children. In 1660 and 1661 he travelled on the Continent, accompanied by his brother Edward, and a tutor. He served in seven Parliaments for Tavistock.

No. 5.   HUGO DE GROOT, OR GROTIUS.

When a boy.   Black dress.   White collar.

BORN 1583.   DIED 1645-6.

BY MIEREVELDT.

BORN at Delft, the son of John de Groot (Dutch for 'Great'), of an ancient family, Burgomaster of the town, and Curator of the recently founded University of Leyden, which was destined to become so famous. Hugo was one day totally to eclipse the fame of his father, though he too was a man of great learning and cultivation. Hugo was remarkable for his proficiency in Latin and Greek when a mere child, and, unlike most precocious geniuses, he fulfilled his early promise. He was placed with an Arminian minister at the Hague, and when only eight years old, composed some Latin verses, which are still extant. At the age of eleven he was entered as a student at Leyden, and became the pet (so to speak) of a circle of learned professors, of whom he was destined to become the foremost. In those early days Hugo distinguished himself in every branch of learning, addressed a Greek ode to the Prince of Orange, which gained him great κῦδος, as did shortly afterwards a Latin poem in honour of Henry the Fourth of France.

In 1598 Hugo accompanied Count Justin of Nassau (natural son of William the Silent) and John Olden Barneveldt on a diplomatic mission to Paris. Henry the Fourth, remembering the tribute paid him by the young foreigner, showed him especial favour, presented him with his picture and a chain of massive gold, and pointed him out to the courtiers as 'a miracle of learning, and the wonder of Holland.' The young Prince of Condé also took great delight in his society, and called him his secretary. To this youthful patron Grotius dedicated his first printed work, *Martianus Capella*.

Hugo remained in Paris for about a year, when a summons from his parents called him home. On his return he took up his abode at the house of Prince Maurice of Nassau's chaplain, a learned and pious man, where he studied law without neglecting his literary labours. He pleaded his first cause at Delft when only seventeen, gaining thereby the greatest applause. He published works on astronomy, physics, navigation, both in dead and living languages, and his description of the siege of Ostend (which place had held out three years against the Spaniards) was considered a masterpiece. His writings on contemporary history, in which he did full justice to the noble and patriotic deeds of his countrymen, also called especial attention to the merits of the young author, and the Government were easily induced to listen to the recommendation of Olden Barneveldt, and in due time Hugo Grotius was selected as historiographer, and this in preference to many candidates, all of whom were his seniors, while the salary was increased in consideration of the nominee's acknowledged talents. The French King wished to secure him as President of the Library at Paris, and the star of Grotius was now in the ascendant. He was named to the post of Pensionary of the city of Rotterdam, vacant by the death of Elias, brother to Olden Barneveldt, with whom Grotius now contracted an intimate friendship. This office, together with other privileges, entitled the holder to a seat in the Assembly of the States of Holland, and afterwards to the same honour in that of the States-General. On this promotion, Grotius's father was desirous that his son should marry, and an alliance was accordingly agreed on with Maria von Reigensberg, a lady of noble family in Zeeland, the daughter of a Burgomaster of Veer, in that province. The bride, it would seem, was by no means comely in appearance; she was stoutly built and of a swarthy complexion, but the future proved Maria von Grotius to be a woman of strong affection, acute intelligence, and indomitable courage. Shortly after his arrival in Rotterdam, Grotius was sent to England on a mission connected with some dispute which had arisen between the Dutch and English, connected with the whale fisheries, and here he was cordially welcomed by James the First, with whom he had many conferences, on matters theological, as well as diplomatic, while his society was eagerly courted by all the men of eminence in this country. But a storm was gathering over the calm horizon of Hugo Grotius's hitherto bright career. On his return to Rotterdam he found that the religious differences which had been gradually waxing hotter and hotter throughout the United Provinces had now assumed a most formidable aspect. The whole country was divided into two separate factions of the Arminians and the Gomarites; the former party strongly opposing, and the latter strenuous upholding, the doctrines of Calvin. After some wavering, or perhaps we had better say investigation, of the subject, Grotius decided on embracing the tenets of Arminius. Remonstrances and counter-remonstrances were brought forward by the two parties, Synods were convened, public disturbances ensued, and the disputes which had commenced in a question of dogma developed into political animosity. A decree was issued by the States, with a view to putting down the serious riots which had lately occurred, and extraordinary powers were granted to magisterial bodies, a measure which, combined with others equally obnoxious to him, gave great offence to Maurice of Nassau, the Stadtholder, and he was violently incensed against the men at whose instigation the step had been taken. Between the prince and the friend of his youth, John Olden Barneveldt, great differences of opinion had for some time existed, and it was in the year 1619 that this venerable patriot and his friend Grotius were both thrown into prison—whence the former, after a summary and unjust trial, only came out on his way to the scaffold. In that solemn moment Barneveldt showed great solicitude as to the fate of his friend, and learning in answer to his question that Grotius did not lie under sentence of death, he exclaimed, 'I greatly rejoice, for he is young, and will, I firmly trust, live long to be of service to his country.' The trial of Grotius followed, and accusations as groundless as those which had been brought forward against the grand Pensionary were laid to his charge, including treason to his country, complicity with Spain, etc. etc., and he was sentenced to imprisonment for life and the confiscation of his entire property. He was conveyed from one prison to another, until the castle of Loevenstein, near Gorcum in South Holland, was chosen for his final resting-place. This gloomy old fortress was considered impregnable, and the most stringent measures were taken against escape; indeed the internal arrangements of the building and its contiguity to the river seemed to preclude all possibility of evasion. Here Grotius and his learned friend Hogersbaert were immured, and by dint of manifold petitions and 'continual wearying,' their faithful wives were allowed to share their captivity. But all intercourse was forbidden between the two men who were attached to each other, not only by friendship, but sympathy in literary pursuits, while the poor ladies were altogether denied the consolation of each other's society; and when Hogersbaert's wife fell ill, Madame Grotius petitioned in vain for the privilege (so dear to every gentle-hearted woman) of ministering to her friend in sickness, or cheering her last moments with the promise of watching over the dying mother's six helpless children. The only proof of sympathy which one captive was allowed to show the other was in the transmission of a pathetic epitaph by Hugo Grotius, which was gratefully received by the unhappy widower.

Madame Grotius had contrived to retain a portion of her

own, when her husband's property was confiscated, and with this small sum she endeavoured to make his condition less intolerable. She rejected with disdain the scanty dole allowed by Government for the maintenance of the prisoner, and constantly ferried over to Gorcum, on the opposite side of the river, to cater for little dainties for her lord, and the noble dame would stand for hours over the kitchen fire preparing the daily banquet for him and for their children. Maria was indeed one of those characters of combined strength and tenderness, which go near to form 'the perfect woman.' When her husband was first arrested, her anxiety for his life never betrayed her into weakness or cowardice; on the contrary, she wrote constantly, urging him to maintain his principles, and rather die than ask pardon, which could only be obtained through servile submission. Her admiration for Grotius, and her pride in his genius, could only be equalled by her affection. To think that a man, with whose name Europe already rang, whose writings were fated to influence the destinies of nations—that he should waste the best days of his life in prison —wither away, as it were, in a living tomb,—the thought was intolerable to her. The Commandant of the fortress, one Deventer, cherished a spite against his noble prisoner, arising from some family feud which had been handed down from the last generation, and he took especial delight in riveting the heavy chains as tightly as he could, and making captivity unbearable. Air and exercise were seldom vouchsafed, and Grotius, the philosopher, the metaphysician, the historian, the world-famed author, might be seen spinning a large top in the lobby adjoining his apartments for the best exercise he could get! Even the society of his beloved wife and that of his children did not suffice to prevent the hours from dragging heavily along, deprived as he was of the joys of a scholar's heart, the books in which he could study the thoughts of others, the writing materials with which he could record his own; therefore Maria never rested until she had wrung from the authorities the permission to obtain from Grotius's own library the volumes most coveted, together with pen, ink, and paper. Henceforth the captive's life was no longer a blank. He devoured his classics, he made notes and translations, he wrote works on History, Theology, Jurisprudence, and thus shed a light on the outer world from behind the walls of his gloomy fortress. But these alleviations were not sufficient to content the faithful wife; she had more daring schemes in view. Had she ever heard, or does the Dutch language, so rich in proverbs, contain an equivalent for our 'Love laughs at locksmiths'? Certain it is she was destined to realise the words of a lowly poet of our own days—

> 'Oh! woman all would do, would dare;
> To save her heart's best cherished care
> She'd roam the world tract wide,
> Nor bolts nor bars can 'gainst her stand,
> Or weapons stay her gentle hand,
>   When love and duty guide.'

She laid her train most carefully, most skilfully, nor did she allow any undue haste to mar its fulfilment. She had in her constant marketings at Gorcum cultivated the acquaintance and gained the friendship of many of the bettermost tradespeople of the town, and her maid Lieschen, who was market-woman in turn, was instructed to do the same. They both talked constantly to the good burghers' wives, and interested them in behalf of the captive, the great writer and philosopher, and, what came nearer the women's hearts, the tender husband and father. The plot was ripening in the devoted conspirator's mind; but there came a moment of suspicion and alarm; it was reported that Madame Grotius had bought a coil of ropes in Gorcum, doubtless to facilitate her husband's escape. An inquiry was instituted, when the suspected lady herself pointed out to the emissaries of justice, that ropes, even wings, could they be procured, would be unavailing in a dungeon where the captive on his entrance had to pass through thirteen different doors, each of which was bolted after him. She had in fact other means in store, and fortune favoured her in one particular, namely, that the cross-grained commandant was summoned to a distant town on military business, and Maria Grotius had already ingratiated herself with Madame Deventer by occasional presents of luxuries, to which the good lady was by no means insensible, such as venison, poultry, and the like. When the books were first allowed to enter the prison walls, the chest was submitted on its entrance and exit to a strict search, which had of late been deemed unnecessary.

Accordingly, one day in the absence of the Governor, Madame Grotius went to call on his wife, who always received her kindly. 'I am come,' she said, 'to ask you to help me. My husband is killing himself, poring over those dreadful folios, and making himself ill. We are both very grateful for the permission granted that he should have the use of his own library, but lately he has been working his brain, and tiring his head over those tremendously heavy volumes, heavy in every sense of the word, I want to send them away, and get others lighter and smaller. Now, of course, your word is as good as that of your husband in his absence. Do me the kindness to order your men to carry down the chest as usual to the water's edge, and not demur because it is extra heavy. I have a perfect spite against those bulky volumes.' The vice-regent of the commandant, 'dressed in a little brief authority,' made use of it to oblige her friend, and gave the order willingly. Maria went back to her own quarters. 'Mother, dear,' said Cornelia, the eldest of her children, 'did you not say to-morrow was the Fair at Gorcum, and that you were told on such occasions even exiles and outlaws might appear in the town? Why should not dear father go there in that case?' Surely out of the child's mouth came a word of wisdom; she little knew that her remark was hailed as an omen by her parents. Maria von Grotius next sent for her maid, and asked her the startling question, 'If we can conceal your master in the book-chest, will you take charge of it to Gorcum, and incur the whole risk?'—which was indeed great. The loving wife would gladly have undertaken the task herself, but she judged it would be more likely to avert suspicion if she remained in the castle. The brave girl pledged herself to carry out the directions of her mistress to the letter, and the two women began their arduous and dangerous preparations. It was the beginning of the week, and the month March 1621, that Grotius rose early and, kneeling down by the side of the empty trunk, prayed fervently for the success of the hazardous enterprise. He was dressed in soft linen and underclothing, and got into the chest, which was only four feet long, and narrow in proportion, he being a tall and strongly built man. His wife helped him to coil himself up, and then placed a large Testament as a pillow for the beloved head, the position of which she arranged so that the mouth should come opposite the small holes she had drilled to admit a little air. She closed the chest and sat on the top for a considerable time, to ascertain if her husband could possibly endure the confinement. Then lifting the lid once more, she knelt down and took a solemn farewell of him she best loved on earth, kissed him tenderly, locked the box, and gave the key to the maid. We can only guess at the feelings of anguish and tenderness which convulsed the heart of that noble woman at that supreme instant. Then she arranged her husband's day-clothes on the chair, with his dressing slippers, and drew the curtains closely round the bed, into which she got hastily. After that she rang the bell, and when the servant who usually waited on them answered the summons, she looked out and said she was so sorry she could not go to Gorcum that day for she was not well herself, and did not like to leave her husband who was very ill; throwing out at the same time a hint that he was feverish, and there might be fear of infection. The servant said it was all the better she should not go, for the river was swollen and the wind was high, and in fact it was almost dangerous. 'That is unfortunate,' she said, 'for my husband resolved that these heavy folios should go to-day; however, my maid is no coward, and she will take charge of them, even if the ferry should be rough.' She then bade him go and summon the soldiers whom Madame Deventer had told off to carry the chest. They came, and on lifting it one of them said, 'I believe the Arminian is inside, it is so confoundedly heavy.'

The poor wife trembling behind the closely drawn curtains made some tame jest about the relative weight of a man and those horrid books, and then the precious load was carried out of the room. But Lieschen had many terrible moments yet to come. The soldiers maintained, nothing but a man could weigh so heavily, and one of them said he would get a gimlet and run it into the Arminian, and another told anecdotes of how malefactors had been smuggled out of prison in a like manner. Poor Lieschen had to jest, while her heart quaked: 'Your gimlet must be a long one,' she said, 'to reach my master in his bedroom in the castle.' Then followed the awful question, whether Madame Deventer would consider it necessary to inspect the contents of the chest, which she fortunately declined. So on the soldiers went, grumbling at their heavy load, and when they arrived at the wharf, the maid entreated that a double plank might be placed to carry the chest on board, for, said she, 'those books are to be returned to a learned Professor, and I shall never be forgiven if any mischance should befall them.' At length the transport was effected, and the large box deposited on the deck beside Lieschen. The river was much swollen, the wind was raging, the vessel heeled over to one side, and the girl had to beseech the skipper to have the box secured with ropes, and down she sat beside it in an agony of terror, both for herself and her precious charge. She then threw a white handkerchief over her head and let the ends flutter in the breeze, the signal that had been agreed on between her and her mistress to show so far all was well and the vessel in motion; for a servant in the castle had added to the women's accumulated terror by predicting that the captain would not embark in such a storm.

The unhappy wife was straining her eyes, dimmed by tears, between the bars of the window, while the maid sat shivering with cold and fear, her head between her hands; and on the top of the chest an officer of the garrison had taken up his post, and drummed and pommelled with his feet against the sides, and she dared not bid him desist from doing so—for what reason could she assign for interference? At last she bethought herself to ask him to get off, as there were not only books but fragile china in the chest, and he might break it by that constant shaking. The longest voyage, like the longest day, will have an end, and surely that voyage from Loevenstein to Gorcum must have seemed like one round the world to the terrified girl; yet her fears did not deaden her woman's wit, and she was always ready with an answer. She bribed the skipper and his son to transport the chest themselves to its destination on a hand-barrow, beside which she walked. 'Do you hear what my boy says?' observed the captain; 'he declares there is some living thing in your trunk, Miss.' 'No doubt,' was the answer, with a forced laugh; 'don't you know that Arminian books are alive, full of motion and spirit?' In this manner the three companions, with the fourth concealed, threaded the dense crowds of the fair at Gorcum, and made their way to a warehouse which Lieschen indicated. It belonged to a well-to-do tradesman (relative of a learned professor, a friend of the prisoner's), and the wife was one of those whom Maria von Grotius frequently visited on her marketing expeditions to Gorcum. The bearers of the chest were exorbitant in their demands, but Lieschen was very anxious to be relieved of their presence, and made little haggling about the price. No sooner had they departed than the poor girl hastened into the shop where the ribbon-dealer and his wife were busy selling their wares, and stepping noiselessly up to the latter, whispered the truth in her astonished ear. The startled Vrouw became deathly pale, and seemed like to faint, but she left the shop with Lieschen, and then what a moment of condensed and mingled hope and terror! Lieschen kneeled down and knocked. 'Master, dear master,' she exclaimed. No answer. 'Oh my God, he is dead,' cried the girl, while her companion stood quaking with terror and calling out it was a bad business. But hark! A feeble cry from the inside, 'Open quick, I was not sure of your voice.' The chest was opened, and Grotius arose, almost as from a tomb. The still terrified shopwoman took Lieschen and her master into an upper room through a trap-door, and then began to tell him how alarmed she was, and that she feared, if he were found, her husband would be imprisoned in his stead, and all their property forfeited. 'No, no,' said Grotius, 'before I got into this trunk I prayed earnestly to God, who has preserved me hitherto, but rather than ruin you and your husband, I would get into the box again, and go back to Loevenstein.' 'Oh no,' said the kind-hearted woman, 'we will do all in our power to serve you'; and off she flew to her brother-in-law, a clothier of Gorcum, whom she found in conversation with the very officer who had been Lieschen's fellow-passenger, and who had annoyed her by sitting on the trunk. Drawing her relative aside, the mercer's wife explained the whole state of the case, and bade him follow her to the warehouse without a moment's delay, when she would introduce him to the fugitive.

The clothier was nothing loath to be instrumental in the escape of a man whom he greatly admired, being himself no mean scholar, and well acquainted with the writings of Grotius, on entering whose presence, he thus addressed him, 'Are you, sir, that man with whose name the whole of Europe is now ringing?'

'I am Hugo Grotius,' was the reply, 'and into your hands I commit my safety and my life.'

No time was lost. The clothier, who was acquainted with every one in Gorcum, found the man he could trust, a mason working on a scaffolding in the town. He beckoned him down, and told him there was an errand of mercy to be performed, to which a large reward was appended, and asked if he would undertake the task. The mason answered in the affirmative, and was then directed to procure a set of workingmen's clothes, which unfortunately proved too scanty for Grotius, and thus occasioned a new difficulty; the trunk-hose and sleeves were too short, the latter revealing the finely shaped white hand, whose hardest labour had hitherto been the work of the pen. The two women had much ado to patch up and lengthen out, and with dirt and clay, putty and plaster, they smeared the hands of the great philosopher, and sent him forth with fear and trembling, to run the gauntlet of many dangers. Next door was a library, which was the resort of learned professors, and book-lovers of all kinds, to many of whom Grotius was known by sight. He slouched his felt hat over his eyes, took his measuring-wand in his hand, and followed the mason through the streets to the bank of the river, where the friendly clothier met them. The weather was still boisterous, and the boatmen refused to ply, till the mason urged on them the necessity he was under of fulfilling a contract for buying stone for a large building at Altona, and assured them he would be a considerable loser by delay. These arguments were backed by the clothier, who put his hand into his pocket, and drew forth the most convincing of all arguments in the eyes of the boatmen. And at length the embarkation was effected; the ferry crossed in safety, and then the two masons walked to a neighbouring town, where they hired a carriage, and entering into confidential talk with the driver, informed him that the taller of the two was a disguised bankrupt flying from his creditors into foreign territory, and this, they said, would account for his wish to avoid observation as they passed through the towns. On went the little carriage, the driver of which was not long before he set down Grotius as a fool who soon 'parted with his money,' for of its value he showed a profound ignorance. In this respect we see that the driver differed in opinion from the rest of the world. They travelled through the night, and on the morrow, arriving early within a few leagues of Antwerp, they were met by a patrol of soldiers, who challenged them, asked for their passport, and inquired to whose service they belonged. Grotius evaded the question, and added jestingly, ' As to my passport, that is in my feet.' They fraternised, and the fugitive had now not only a military escort, but a good horse provided for his own riding; and in this manner entered the city of Antwerp. He alighted at the house of a banished friend, who proved to be in great anxiety on account of his wife's illness, so the daughter of the family informed him; but no sooner did her parents learn the name of their unexpected visitor, than not only the master of the house, but the invalid herself hastened down to bid him welcome. The meeting was indeed a happy one, and although secrecy was deemed prudent, yet the news spread among a few compatriots, under the same sentence of proscription, who all flocked to the house, where a joyous little banquet was prepared, at which the illustrious journeyman mason, still in his working clothes, presided. Conversation flowed, and glasses clinked merrily that night to the health of Grotius and his gallant Maria, not forgetting the brave and faithful handmaiden. In the meantime how went affairs at Loevenstein? Madame Grotius had given out that her husband's illness was infectious; but no sooner was she apprised of his safety, than she laughed her gaoler and his guards to scorn. 'Here is the cage,' she said merrily, 'but the bird has flown!' The commandant rained curses on her head, and increased the rigour of her imprisonment. He went across the river to browbeat the good shopwoman and her husband, but all this fuming and fretting did not bring back the prisoner. Madame Grotius sent a petition to the States-General and to the Stadtholder, to which neither were insensible. It was on this occasion that Prince Maurice (who was not wont to measure his words) made the ungallant speech—'I thought that *black pig* would outwit us.' We can fancy he said it with a grim smile, for very shortly afterwards Madame Grotius found herself at liberty, with the permission to carry away all that belonged to her in Loevenstein. Grotius, on his part, addressed a letter to the States-General before leaving Antwerp, in which he maintained that he had done his duty as Pensionary of Rotterdam, in the measures he had advocated, thereby incurring their censure, and he proceeded at length to propound his political views, and to offer suggestions for the restoration and maintenance of internal peace, concluding by justifying the means he had used for escape, having employed 'neither violence nor corruption.' And he furthermore declared that the persecutions he had suffered, and the hardships to which he had been exposed, could never diminish his love for his country, for whose prosperity he devoutly prayed.

Grotius remained some time at Antwerp, and then determined on proceeding to France, where his wife and family were allowed to join him; and Lieschen, good, brave Lieschen, who would not rejoice to hear that her fate was one usually reserved for the last page of a story-book—'she lived happy ever afterwards,' becoming the wife of her faithful fellow-servant, who had learned the rudiments of law from his master during their captivity,—a study which the good man continued on leaving Loevenstein, and rose step by step until he became a thriving and respected advocate in the tribunals of Holland.

But to return to Grotius : On his arrival in Paris he was kindly received by the French King, who granted him a provisional pension (very uncertain, by the way, in payment). In a pleasant country-house which had been lent him, in the environs of Senlis, he resumed his literary labours with great assiduity, working first at his 'Apology,' which he wrote in his mother-tongue, and sent off to Holland as soon as completed. This was a full and detailed exposition of the motives which had actuated his conduct, and of his religious and political sentiments. It produced the greatest possible excitement in Holland. The Government designated it as a foul and slanderous libel, reflecting on the honour of the States, of the Stadtholder, and all manner of bodies magisterial and municipal. The publication was interdicted, and every person forbidden, on pain of death, to retain it in their possession. In the meantime the 'Apology' was published, and eagerly read in Paris, and Grotius now set to work on his famous treatise on the Rights of Peace and War.

The pretty country-house in which he lived was the resort of men of letters, and among his frequent visitors was the learned De Thou, who gave him the free use of his valuable library. In 1625, on the death of Prince Maurice, the exile wrote to the new Stadtholder, Frederic Henry, asking permission to return, but without success. He then sent his wife into Holland, and through her judicious management and the exertions of his friends, the reversal of the decree of confiscation was obtained, and his property and effects were restored to him. At length he ventured back to his own country in person, and first proceeded to Rotterdam, where he was cordially received in private, but the authorities would not sanction his appearance in public, and the same reception awaited him at Amsterdam and Delft. The States-General, of whom he disdained to ask pardon ('for,' said he, 'in what have I offended?') were exasperated at his boldness in venturing back without permission, and orders were given to seize his person, and give notice to the Government, while a reward of 2000 florins was offered for his capture; but Grotius was too much beloved; no one was found to betray him. Still his position was undoubtedly perilous, and joining his wife on her return from Zeeland, they took up their abode for the summer and winter in or near the town of Hamburg.

Grotius was now overwhelmed with proposals of employment, and overtures of all descriptions from foreign powers—Spain, Poland, the Duchy of Holstein, and the hero Gustavus Adolphus, King of Sweden, for whom our philosopher had the profoundest veneration. With this monarch's envoy at the French Court, Benedict Oxenstiern, a relative of the celebrated Chancellor, Grotius had formed an intimate friendship, and when they were both residing at Frankfort, they became almost inseparable. The King of Sweden died, and was succeeded by his daughter, the eccentric Christina, whose admiration for the fame of Grotius even exceeded that of her father. Through the medium of Oxenstiern she made him numerous offers, but Grotius declined all but one employment. He volunteered to return to Paris as the Swedish Ambassador, provided the Queen would allow him a sufficient salary to maintain his position as her representative, which nomination was most distasteful to Richelieu, who was then Prime Minister. But after a time his opposition was overruled, and Grotius made his public entry into the French capital, where the crooked and tortuous policy pursued by Richelieu, and continued by his successor, Cardinal Mazarin, was most distasteful to Christina's envoy, added to which he was weary of politics, diplomacy, and Court life, and earnestly solicited his recall. Christina acquiesced in the demand, but desired him to repair to Stockholm, where she joined him. Her Majesty did all in her power by promises of provision and favour for himself, his wife, and family, to induce Grotius to become a resident in her country. But he withstood all her tempting offers. Many difficulties to his departure were thrown in his way, but at last he embarked on a vessel bound for Lubeck. He had not been long at sea before a tremendous storm arose, and after three days continual tossing, and constant danger of shipwreck, the passengers landed on the coast of Pomerania, about fourteen miles from Dantzig. Grotius was far from well when he left Stockholm; the climate had proved too cold for him. He had been very ill on the voyage, and after travelling sixty miles in an open wagon, exposed to violent wind and rain, he arrived at Rostock in a most enfeebled condition. No sooner had he arrived than he sent for the doctor and the clergyman, who thus describes his interview in a letter: 'If you are anxious to know how that Phœnix of literature, Hugo Grotius, behaved in his last moments, I will tell you. He sent for me at night. I found him almost at the point of death, and told him how deeply I regretted that I had never seen him in health, to benefit by his conversation. "God has ordered it otherwise," he said. I then bade him prepare for a happier life; to acknowledge and repent his sins, and, chancing to allude to the Pharisee and the publican, "I am that publican," he exclaimed. When I told him to have recourse to Jesus Christ, without whom is no salvation, he answered: "In Him alone I place my trust." Then I repeated aloud the German prayer that begins, "Herr Jesu." He followed in a low voice with clasped hands. I inquired if he understood all, and he said, "Quite well." I continued to read passages of the Word of God for dying persons.' Thus expired this great and good man, far from the kindred he loved, his heart still true to the country which had rejected and expelled him, his deathbed watched by strangers. His body was embalmed and transported to his native city of Delft, where it was interred with great pomp by his fellow-citizens, who at first proposed to erect a statue in his honour, similar to that of Erasmus at Rotterdam, but the idea was abandoned. It was reserved for his descendants to raise a monument to his memory in the said church. We transcribe the modest epitaph written by Grotius on himself—

GROTIUS HIC HUGO EST, BATAVUM CAPTIVUS, ET EXUL
LEGATUS REGNY REGNI SUECIS MAGNAFUI.

No. 6. THE HONOURABLE ANDREW NEWPORT.

In armour. Light brown sleeves. Rich lace cravat. Long hair.

BORN 1622, DIED 1699.

BY SIR GODFREY KNELLER.

E was the son of Lord Newport, the noted Royalist, by Rachel, daughter of Sir John Levison, Knight, of Harington, County Kent, and sister of Sir Richard Levison, Knight of the Bath, of Trentham, County Stafford. Andrew was Commissioner of Customs to Charles the Second. He was M.P. for Shrewsbury from 1689 to 1698. Died unmarried, and was buried at Wroxeter. He bequeathed his manor of Dythan, County Montgomery, and other estates in the same county, and in that of Salop, to his nephew Richard, Lord Newport, son of Francis, Earl of Bradford. Lord Clarendon, in his *History of the Civil Wars*, makes frequent mention of Andrew Newport.

No. 9.

THOMAS WENTWORTH, EARL OF STRAFFORD, AND HIS SECRETARY.

Black dress.

BORN 1594, EXECUTED 1641.

AFTER VANDYCK.

HE eldest son of Sir William Wentworth of Wentworth Wodehouse, County York, by Anne Atkinson of Stowel, County Gloucester. He succeeded his father in his large estates when only twenty-one, being already the husband of 'a fair wife.'

Shortly after his succession he was elected M.P. for York and *Custos Rotulorum* in place of Lord Savile, superseded on account of misconduct, an office from which the Duke of Buckingham requested him to retire that Lord Savile might be reinstated, a proceeding which nettled the high spirit of Sir Thomas, who wrote a refusal so indignant as to make a lifelong enemy of the favourite.

Until the accession of Charles the First, Wentworth, although a silent member of the House of Commons, was a zealous advocate of the Liberal party and a strenuous opposer of the encroachments of the Court. Through the instrumentality of Buckingham he was disqualified from voting by having the post of High Sheriff thrust upon him, and he was soon after summarily dismissed from his office of *Custos Rotulorum*. In the ensuing year he was summoned before the Council and sentenced to imprisonment for refusing to contribute to a loan (levied without the consent of Parliament), on which occasion he made a noble speech expressing his loyalty to the person of Charles the First and his desire to serve him in any way consistent with his duty to his country. On his release from prison he became a strong leader of the Opposition and an eloquent advocate of the famous 'Petition of Rights,' to which the King was compelled to yield his unwilling consent. Then suddenly came the adoption of that line of conduct, so differently judged and so differently accounted for by different biographers. Wentworth declared his conviction that the nation might now be content with the concessions made by the Crown, bade adieu to the party of the 'Pyms and the Prynnes,' walked over to the other side of the House and offered his services, head, heart, and sword, to the royal cause. By some he was termed a traitor, a time-server, an apostate, while others upheld the conduct of a man who chose the moment of impending danger to rally round the unsteady throne and the unpopular sovereign. Charles naturally received him with open arms, and loaded him with favours; but his old ally, Pym, meeting him one day, uttered these ominous words, 'You are going to leave us, but I will never leave you while you have a head on your shoulders'; words too cruelly redeemed.

The murder of the Duke of Buckingham made way for Wentworth's advancement. Raised to the peerage by the title of Viscount Wentworth, he was appointed Lord-Deputy and Commander-in-Chief in Ireland, and sailed for that 'distressful country' with a code for his own government, drawn up by himself, in his pocket, from which he never swerved. Lord Wentworth's administration of Irish affairs, his transient popularity, his reforms in matters civil, military, and religious, his quarrels with the Irish nobles, his punctilio in minute questions of form and ceremony, his hurried voyages to and from England, are subjects intimately connected with the history of the times, but too lengthy to be detailed here. It would have been well for the Lord-Deputy if he had taken the advice of his lifelong friend and correspondent, Archbishop Laud, and had curbed his impetuosity on many occasions.

In 1639 he crossed to England, was created Earl of Strafford, gained the title of Lord-Lieutenant of Ireland, was received into the King's full confidence, and was for a time virtually Prime Minister. Not content with advocating the necessities of raising subsidies, he contributed £20,000 from his own privy purse (as an example to the nation) towards the impending war with Scotland. In spite of ill health and increasing infirmities, Strafford crossed and recrossed St. George's Channel to attend to his duties on either side; the last time in a terrible storm, and nearly died at Chester, on his road to London. Yet his indomitable spirit would not yield. He joined the King at York, and found the army in a sad plight, all hope and spirit fled, and the royal cause 'in the dust.' He became the real, though not the nominal, Commander-in-chief, and although unable to walk, and scarcely able to sit upright on his saddle, Strafford rallied the troops, upbraided the sluggishness of the leaders, and set a brilliant example of energy and courage. But the King stayed his hand and thwarted his activity, loud all the while in his praises, and giving him the Garter. Charles also insisted that they should travel together to London, a proceeding to which Strafford was strongly opposed,—two victims hastening to their doom.

A few days after the opening of Parliament Pym began his long-meditated attack on his former friend—the blood-hounds were on the track, the hunt was up. Our limited space forbids us to do more than glance at the circumstances of Strafford's arrest and trial, but in truth it is a well-known tale. He was impeached by Pym of high treason, compelled to listen to the charge on his knees, was given into custody, and lodged in the Tower. There is extant a most graphic description of the scene which Westminster Hall presented on the occasion of the trial, crowded to the roof, the King and Queen being present, and the whole court and nobility of England, ladies of the highest rank, whose tears flowed copiously, and whose verdict was unanimous in favour of the illustrious prisoner. It was well said by the elder Disraeli, that 'Strafford's eloquence was so great as to perpetuate the sympathy which he received in the hour of his agony.' He had indeed need of his eloquence. Every obstacle was thrown in his way, especially in the matter of summoning witnesses, while his personal enemies were invited from all parts of the country. His confidence was betrayed, his words perverted, the whole proceedings were unlawful and unprecedented, and the Solicitor-General heaped insults on the accused. A Bill of Attainder was provided, and the few individuals who gave negative votes had their names posted up in the City as Straffordians.

There was a passage of arms between the two Houses on the subject, but the vultures were hovering round, and would not be disappointed of their prey. Thomas Wentworth, Earl of Strafford, was declared guilty of high treason. On this sad passage, the saddest of all in Charles's sad life, we need not dwell long. He had pledged his royal word to his noble friend, 'You shall not suffer in honour, in fortune, or in life.' Yet after some hesitation and delay, weeping all the time, he signed the death-warrant, laying up for himself hours of deep remorse during the few years he survived. The generous prisoner wrote to his master, indeed, to absolve him from his promise; but when he learned he was to prepare for death, he raised his eyes to heaven exclaiming, 'Put not your trust in princes, or in any child of man.'

Entrance Hall. 41

During the short interval between the sentence and the execution, the captive busied himself in settling his worldly affairs, writing wise, tender, and pathetic letters to his relatives, and devoting his mind to the fulfilment of his religious duties.

An earnest request to be allowed to visit his attached friend and fellow-prisoner, Archbishop Laud, was cruelly refused, and he was only permitted to send him a message, entreating the prelate's blessing as he passed to execution. Accordingly, on the 12th of May 1641, Strafford, on his way to the scaffold, raised his eyes to the window of the cell where the Archbishop was confined, and perceived the aged and trembling hand waving through the bars a solemn farewell to the man he had so long and so faithfully loved. Thousands of spectators lined the streets, the passions of the mob had been so excited against the prisoner that the guards kept close to the carriage lest he should be torn to pieces. Strafford smiled calmly, and remarked it would matter little to him whether he died by the hands of the executioner or by those of the people. 'He had faced death too often to fear it in any shape.'

. His friend, Archbishop Ussher, and his brother, Sir George Wentworth, were already on the platform. Strafford spoke for some time. He declared that his whole aim through life had been the joint and individual prosperity of the King and the people, although he had had the misfortune to be misconstrued. He denied all the charges brought against him, asked forgiveness of all men he had injured, and prayed 'that we may all meet eternally in heaven, where sad thoughts shall be driven from our hearts, and tears wiped from our eyes.' Then he bade farewell to those near him, embracing his brother, by whom he sent tender messages to his wife and children. 'One stroke,' he said, 'will make my wife husbandless, my children fatherless, my servants masterless; but let God be to you and to them all in all.' Taking off his doublet, he thanked God he could do so as cheerfully as ever he did when going to bed. Then he forgave the executioner and all the world. It was indeed an imposing scene,—Strafford on that momentous day apparently restored to all the energy of health and vigour, his symmetrical form, his regular features, with a complexion 'pallid but manly.' Once more he knelt in prayer between the Archbishop and the Minister, tried the block, and having warned the executioner that he would give the sign, stretched forth his white and beautifully formed hands, which Vandyck has immortalised, which Henrietta Maria, his sworn enemy, had pronounced the finest in the world; and one stroke from the cruel axe ended the mortal career of Thomas, Earl of Strafford.

He was thrice married,—first, to Lady Margaret Clifford, who died childless; secondly, to Lady Arabella Holles, daughter to the Earl of Clare, by whom he had one son and two daughters; and thirdly, to Elizabeth, daughter of Sir Godfrey Rhodes (the marriage was a clandestine one), from whom he was separated for a period immediately after the ceremony, and it was some time before he would acknowledge her openly; in fact a mystery hung over the whole matter. Lord Strafford's letters to this lady during his trial were couched in affectionate terms. She bore him several children, one of whom alone survived him. Of his connection with that beautiful schemer, Lady Carlisle, born Percy, there can be no doubt,—'she who,' says Sir Philip Warwick, 'changed her gallant from Strafford to Pym, thus going over to his deadly enemy'; but there were many other names coupled with that of Lord Strafford, apparently without any reason, save the love of slander.

No. 10.
COLONEL THE HONOURABLE JOHN RUSSELL.
Brown embroidered dress. *Wig.*

DIED 1681.
By Sir Godfrey Kneller.

E was the youngest son of Francis, fourth Earl of Bedford, by Catherine Bridges. He served with distinction in the royal army under Charles the First, and at the Restoration was appointed Colonel of the first regiment of the Foot Guards. At one time there were negotiations carrying on for his marriage with a daughter of the Earl of Bath, which was prevented by the young lady's family, who were desirous she should marry her cousin, heir to the Earldom of Bath. The gallant colonel then became a suitor for the hand of the famous beauty La Belle Hamilton. There is a laughable description of him in the *Memoires de Grammont*, and we cannot but think that as the chronicler himself carried off the prize, he might have been rather more generous in his delineation of an unsuccessful rival:

'M. Le Colonel Russell avoit bien soixante ans, son courage et sa fidélité l'avoient distingué dans les guerres civiles. Il n'y avoit pas longtemps qu'on avoit quitté le ridicule, des chapeaux pointus, pour tomber dans l'autre extrémité. Le vieux Russell, effraié d'une chute si terrible, voulut prendre un milieu qui le rendit remarquable. Il l'étoit encore par la constance envers les pourpoints taillardés qu'il a soutenus longtemps après leur suppression universelle. Mais ce qui surprenoit le plus c'étoit un certain mélange d'avarice et de libéralité sans cesse en guerre l'une avec l'autre, depuis qu'il y étoit avec l'amour.'

He was selected by his nephew, Lord Russell, to carry the noble letter which the prisoner had written from Newgate on the 19th July 1683 to the King.

No. 11. FRANCIS RUSSELL, FOURTH EARL OF BEDFORD.

Black dress.

DIED 1641.

BY REMÉE.

E was the only son of William Russell, called the Heroic Baron of Thornhaugh, whom he accompanied to Ireland when only nine years old. A curious picture at Woburn leads us to believe that the young Francis shared his father's love of sport, being there represented in a white hunting jacket with green hose, a hawk on his hand, and two dogs in couples beside him. He was knighted in 1604 by James the First, at Whitehall, and the ensuing year he married Catherine, daughter and co-heir of Gyles Brydges, third Lord Chandos, with whom he lived very happily; and during the first years of his marriage he devoted himself to domestic life, and took great delight in study. Having received a legal education he prosecuted his researches into questions of law, parliamentary privileges and the like, which were destined to prove useful to him in his public career. He succeeded his father, as Baron Thornhaugh, in 1613; and his cousin, Edward Russell, in the Earldom of Bedford in 1627. He frequented the society of such men as Sir Robert Cotton, Selden, Eliott, and was ever ready, says

one of his biographers, to uphold the liberty of the subject against such despots as James the First. On the accession of Charles the First, Lord Bedford continued the same independent line of conduct, and several times fell under the displeasure of the Court. In 1628 he distinguished himself by his steadfast advocacy of the famous Petition of Rights (to which Charles was in the end compelled to give an unwilling consent); and he received in consequence the royal commands to betake himself to the distant county of Devonshire, of which he was Lord-Lieutenant. Both political bias and private friendship attached him to the so-called popular party, which laid down as their principle for action 'to prescribe limits to the monarchical power.' The profession of such opinions naturally led to the fact that Lord Bedford, among many others, became an object of suspicion to the Court. A rumour was set on foot that he had been instrumental in the circulation of a seditious pamphlet, and on this plea he was arrested and imprisoned for a short time. In 1630 he took a prominent part in the drainage of the Fens in the centre of England, including the counties of North Hants, Lincoln, Hunts, Bedford, Cambridge, and Norfolk; called the Great Level, and subsequently in his honour the Bedford Level. In 1637 this generous and public-minded man had expended for his own share of this great work £100,000, but he was not destined to witness its completion. The part that Lord Bedford took in the political events of the day—in the struggles between King and Parliament, in the differences with the Scots—is not all this written in the chronicles of the civil wars of Charles the First's disastrous reign? Suffice it to say that some of the popular Lords, and Lord Bedford in particular, became aware of the advisability of moderation, and the necessity of curbing the headlong opposition of the popular party. But we cannot do better than to quote the eloquent words of the great historian Lord Clarendon (then

Mr. Hyde). He says: 'This Lord was the person of the greatest interest in the whole party, being of the best estate and best understanding, and therefore most likely to govern the rest.' He was also of great civility and good-nature, and though occasionally hot-tempered, and for the moment impatient of contradiction, yet his opinions were wise and moderate. He was a good adviser to the King, and served him in the end far better than many who cajoled and flattered him. Lord Bedford was a man of strict religion, and withstood the attempt to evict the bishops from the Upper House. He with many others of the same party were sworn of the Privy Council, and in this manner gained Charles's ear, and exercised some degree of influence over him in regulating and modifying measures that appeared prejudicial to the common good. He was selected to be one of the Lords Commissioners sent to confer with the Scots in the hope to compose the long-existing differences. The King liked to transact business with him, and was inclined to listen to his suggestions as to persons fitted to be appointed to offices of state. Indeed Charles pressed upon Lord Bedford himself the post of Lord Treasurer, 'which the Bishop of London was as willing to lay down as any one else could be to take up,' but Lord Bedford refused the office. He was one of the few Peers (to his honour be it spoken) who exerted himself to the utmost to save the life of Lord Strafford. He pleaded his cause vainly with his colleague, the Earl of Essex; and finding him inexorable, prevailed on Mr. Hyde (in a long interview he had on the subject) to intercede with Lord Essex. He also endeavoured to keep the King up to his original intention of commuting or mitigating the sentence. He observed to Mr. Hyde that he thought 'the Earl of Strafford's business was a rock on which they would all split, and that he was sure the passion of Parliament would undo the kingdom.'

But a sudden attack of illness arrested Lord Bedford's

useful and noble career. He was seized with the small-pox, and on ascertaining the fact, his first step was to send away his daughter, Lady Brooke, lest she should fall a victim to the fell disease which wrought such havoc in the house of Russell, seeing that his son and great-grandson both died of the same. Lord Bedford was very much averse to the treatment which his physician, Dr. Cragg, prescribed for him, namely, to be kept a close prisoner to his bed. And when forbidden to get up, he sighed dolefully and said, ' Well, then, I must die to observe your rules.'

Dr. Cademan, a medical man who had advocated a different treatment, published a pamphlet, which gave as his opinion that Lord Bedford 'had died of too much bed, rather than of the small-pox.' The same authority, speaking of the Earl's devotion, says : ' I never saw the like, though I have waited upon many who had no other business left but to die well. Commending his body to be buried with decency, but without pomp, his breath was spent before his hands and eyes ceased to be lifted up to Heaven, as if his soul would have carried his body along with it.'

So passed away on the 9th of May 1641 Francis Russell, called the wise Earl of Bedford, a loss to the unfortunate Strafford, whose sentence was carried out in a few days ; a loss to the King, whose wholesome adviser he was ; a loss to the popular party, whose violence he would fain have curbed. His death was universally mourned, and every mark of respect paid to his memory. Three hundred coaches with Peers and their servants attended ; a long and solemn procession followed the body on its road to Chenies, the burying-place of the Russell family, with led horses, banners displayed, Garter King-at-Arms, 'all the pomp of heraldry and pride of power'; and this great and good man was interred amid the prayers and tears of a large multitude. His widow survived him some years, and was then buried beside him.

No. 13.   WILLIAM, LORD RUSSELL.

In armour.   Long flowing hair.

BORN 1639, EXECUTED 1683.

BY RUSSELL.

E was born second son of William, fifth Earl, afterwards first Duke, of Bedford. He went with his elder brother, Lord Russell, to Cambridge, and later travelled in his company, and that of a learned tutor on the Continent. At Augsburg the brothers separated, and William proceeded to Lyons, whence his letters home proved he amused himself very much, and amidst a gay and brilliant society formed a close acquaintance with the eccentric and celebrated ex-Queen, Christina of Sweden, who appeared to have gained great influence over the young Englishman, who evinced a great inclination for some time to enter the Swedish army as a volunteer. His letters during his sojourn in France, many of which were addressed to his tutor, to whom he was much attached, do him honour. When *en route* for England he fell sick at Paris, and finding himself, as he writes, 'at the gates of death,' he assures his old friend that he prays constantly to God to 'give me grace that I may employ in His service the life His mercy has spared to me.'

On his arrival at home, William for a time devoted himself to the care of his brother, then in ill-health, and to giving his father assistance in domestic affairs. At the Restoration, Lord Bedford and his family were marked out for favour, and the Earl carried the sceptre at the Coronation, and soon after William was elected member for Tavistock. Handsome, accomplished, and nobly born, he became a shining light at the brilliant Court of Charles the Second, but his tastes were too earnest, and his bias too virtuous to find any lasting satisfaction in a society so frivolous and immoral. An early attachment to a good and beautiful woman proved a strong safeguard to the young courtier, which was crowned about the year 1669, by a marriage, the happiness of which family and historical records can vouch. It was indeed a well-assorted union, the commencement of 'domestic bliss,' as the poet says, 'the only happiness which has survived the Fall.' William Russell's choice was Rachel, the daughter of the noble loyalist, Thomas Wriothesley, Earl of Southampton, and the daughter-in-law of the Earl of Carbery, being the widow of his eldest son, Lord Vaughan. We refer our readers to our sketch of Lady Russell's life, who retained her widowed title of Lady Vaughan until the death of William's elder brother. In the meantime he began his political career by a zealous and conscientious attention to his parliamentary duties, and was not long before he incurred the lasting animosity of the Duke of York, and indeed of the King himself, by his zealous opposition to many arbitrary measures proposed by the Court party, which, in Russell's opinion, were calculated to endanger 'the liberty of the subject, the safety of the kingdom, and the welfare of the Protestant religion.' In 1679 he was made a Privy Councillor, a dignity he did not long enjoy, for we read shortly after 'that the Lords Russell, Cavendish, and others, finding the King's heart and head were against popular councils, and that their presence in Council could no longer prevent pernicious measures, and not being willing to serve him against the interests of their country, went to him together, and desired him to excuse their attendance any more at Council.' The King gladly accepted their resignation, for he wanted men who would promote his arbitrary measures, and thus, says Smollett, 'Lord Russell, one of the most popular and virtuous men of the nation, quitted the Council Board.'

He was a prominent promoter of the Bill of Exclusion to

prevent the Duke of York, or any Papist whatsoever, from succeeding to the Throne. When the Bill passed the Commons, it was Lord Russell who carried it in person to the Upper House, on which occasion he made a most eloquent speech, and wound up by saying that in the event of changes so occurring, he should be prevented living a Protestant, it was his fixed resolution to die one. But all opposition to the Papal succession was unavailing, and in 1681 the King dissolved Parliament, by which means Lord Russell found himself at liberty for a short space to indulge in the retirement and pleasures of a happy home with the wife and children he adored. But his country's welfare was ever paramount in his mind, and he kept up his interest in public affairs.

During the ensuing summer the Prince of Orange visited England, and had several interviews and confidential conversations with Lord Russell, who, moreover, made himself doubly obnoxious to the Court party by meeting the Duke of Monmouth in his progress through the North, at the head of a considerable body of men.

In conversation with his domestic chaplain Lord Russell once remarked that he was convinced he should one day fall a sacrifice, since arbitrary government could never be set up in England while he lived to oppose it, and that to the last drop of his blood. And it was evident he took little pains to prevent the fulfilment of his own prophecy. This was a period of plots and counter-plots. There had been much talk lately of a Popish plot, and now the Protestant, or Rye House Plot, was said to have been discovered, the object of which, it was affirmed, was to seize the persons of the King and Duke of York on their return from Newmarket. The enemies of Lord Russell, and several other noblemen, who participated in his political views, were glad to take hold of any pretext to secure the ruin of the men on whose downfall they were bent, and many of the highest of England's nobility were now loudly accused of being implicated in the conspiracy, and orders were issued for their arrest. The Duke of Monmouth was not forthcoming, but Lord Russell, strong in his own innocence, refused to make his escape, though strongly urged to do so by many of his friends. He disdained the notion of flight, though from the beginning he gave himself up for lost. So he sat calmly in his study awaiting the arrival of the officers, to whom he made no resistance, and was conveyed first to the Tower and thence to Newgate.

Lord Essex was the next so-called conspirator apprehended, and he also refused every argument for flight, saying that he considered his own life not worth saving, if by drawing suspicion on Lord Russell, so valuable a life as his, also should be endangered. The Duke of Monmouth had it conveyed to Lord Russell that he would willingly give himself up and share his fate. But the noble prisoner answered it would be no advantage to him that his friends should suffer, and so, on the 13th of July 1683, William, Lord Russell, stood at the bar of the Old Bailey on a charge of high treason. That very morning the Lord Essex, who was only a prisoner of three days' standing, was found dead in the Tower with his throat cut. This strange and melancholy event gave rise to conflicting rumours. Many people were of opinion that there had been foul play, and Evelyn was as surprised as he was grieved, 'My Lord Essex being so well known to me as a man of sober and religious deportment.' The news coming to Westminster Hall on the very day of Lord Russell's trial, was said to have had no little influence on the verdict which the jury returned. The prisoner's demeanour during his examination was marked by calm dignity and absence of any sign of agitation, though he occasionally expostulated against the injustice with which the proceedings were carried on. Being asked how he wished to be tried, he replied, 'By God and my country.' Alas ! alas ! the voices of Justice and of

Mercy were alike unheard in the courts of law that day. The prisoner represented that he had been kept in ignorance, until the moment of his appearing at the bar, of the nature of the charges which were to be brought against him, and that he was allowed no time to select his own counsel, etc. etc. He asked permission to employ the hand of another to take notes of the evidence, upon which the Attorney-General (resolved to deprive him of the help of any counsel) churlishly replied, he might have one of his own servants to assist him. 'Then,' said Lord Russell, 'the only assistance I will ask is that of the lady beside me.' At these words, says a contemporary writer, 'a thrill of anguish passed through the court' —a moment of intense pathos, the frequent and glowing records of which, by poet, painter, and historian, pale before the vivid colouring of the fact itself: the noble prisoner turning in his hour of utmost need to the gentle helpmate beside him, his servant, in the literal acceptation of the word —for who could love or serve him better? Rachel, Lady Russell, rose with a calm she had borrowed from her husband's example. Crushing down and stifling the varied emotions of sorrow, indignation, and apprehension, forcing back the rising tears lest they should dim the vision of the scribe, clenching the small white hand to restore its requisite steadiness, Rachel stood motionless for an instant, with every eye upon her—the cold scrutiny of the cruel judges, the inquisitive stare of false friends and perjured witnesses,— while the Attorney-General, in a more subdued tone of voice, said, 'As the lady pleases.' She then with a firm step left her husband's side, and took up her post at the table below. That picture still remains stamped on the memory of her countrymen through the lapse of more than two centuries, and many who only half remember the details of that remarkable trial, and its undoubted importance as regards subsequent events, still bear in mind the touching

Entrance Hall.

episode of the beautiful secretary, the faithful servant, the devoted wife and widow of William, Lord Russell. The jury were not long in returning the verdict of Guilty,—'an act,' says Rapin, 'of the most crying injustice that ever was perpetrated in England.'

To the cruel and hideous sentence for the execution of 'a traitor,' which was read aloud in English (instead of Latin) by his own desire, the prisoner listened with that decency and composure, 'which,' Burnet tells us, 'characterised his whole behaviour during the trial; even as if the issue were a matter of indifference to him.' The result of the proceedings produced an intense excitement. The most strenuous efforts were made in all quarters to save Lord Russell's life both at home and abroad. It was intimated to the King that M. de Ruvigny, a kinsman of Lady Russell's in favour at the Court of France, was coming over with a special message from Louis the Fourteenth to intercede for the prisoner; but Charles was said to have answered with cruel levity that he should be 'happy to receive M. de Ruvigny, but that Lord Russell's head would be off before he arrived.' Many men of position and influence waited on the King in person, and argued with him on the bad effect the execution would produce in many quarters. The Duchess of Portsmouth had a large sum of money offered to secure her interference, but all in vain. Then Lord Russell's 'noble consort' cast herself at the King's feet, and adjured him, by the memory of her father, the loyal and gallant Southampton, to let his services atone for 'the errors into which honest but mistaken principles had seduced her husband.' This was the last instance of female weakness, if it deserve the name, into which Rachel Russell was betrayed. But Charles was inexorable. He whose weak heart was too easily swayed by beauty, too frequently overcome by emotion of a baser kind, remained impervious to

54   *Biographical Catalogue.*

the tears and anguish of this lovely and virtuous woman.
Even the scanty mercy of a short respite was denied her.
She rose from her knees, collected her courage, and from
that moment she fortified herself against the fatal blow, and
endeavoured by her example to strengthen the resolution of
her husband. 'She gave me no disturbance,' was one of the
touching tributes he paid her. Lord Cavendish sent a pro-
position to the prisoner offering to facilitate his escape, even
to change clothes with him, and remain in his stead; but
Lord Russell returned a firm though grateful refusal, con-
sidering the plan impracticable, unlawful, and dangerous to
his faithful friend, and so prepared quietly and calmly for
the end, expressing his conviction that the day of his execution would not be so disturbing to him as the day of his
trial. The time allotted to him was short. He occupied
himself much in writing. He addressed a letter to the King,
which he intrusted to his uncle, Colonel John Russell, to
deliver to Charles immediately after the execution; a noble
and temperate letter, in which the writer hopes his Majesty
will excuse the presumption of an attainted man. He asks
pardon for anything he might have said or done that looked
like a want of respect to the King or duty to the Government. He acquits himself of all designs (and goes on to
declare his ignorance of any such) against either King or
Government. 'Yet I do not deny that I have heard many
things, and said some, contrary to my duty, for which I have
asked God's pardon, and do now humbly beg your Majesty's.
I take the liberty to add *that though I have met with hard
measure, yet I forgive all concerned in it, from the highest to the
lowest;* and I pray God to bless your person and government, and that the public peace and the true Protestant
religion may be preserved under you; and I crave leave to
end my days with this sincere protestation, that my heart
was ever devoted to that which I thought was your true

interest, in which, if I was mistaken, I hope that your displeasure will end with my life, and that no part of it shall fall on my wife and children, being the last petition that will ever be offered from your Majesty's most faithful, most dutiful, and most obedient servant, RUSSELL.

'NEWGATE, *July* 19, 1683.'

He further drew up a long and detailed defence and explanation of his whole conduct, to be given by his own hands to the Sheriffs on the scaffold,—a precious record, preserved in letters of gold among the most cherished archives at Woburn, the scene of the noble writer's youth and childhood.

The evening before his death, after bidding adieu to some of his friends, his wife and children came to take a last farewell. He parted with them (tender father and devoted husband as he was) in composed silence, and Lady Russell had such control over herself that when she was gone he said, 'The bitterness of death is past.' 'He talked,' says Burnet, 'at much length about her. It had rather grieved him that she had run about so much beating every bush for his preservation, but that, perhaps, it would be a mitigation of her sorrow to feel she had done all in her power to save him.' 'Yet,' he said, ' what a blessing it was that she had that magnanimity of spirit joined to her tenderness as never to have desired him to do a base thing for the saving of his own life; there was a signal providence of God in giving him such a wife, with birth, fortune, understanding, religion, and great kindness to him. But her carriage in his extremity was above all! It was a comfort to leave his children in such a mother's hands, who had promised him to take care of herself for his sake.' Burnet further tells us that 'the prisoner received the Sacrament from Archbishop Tillotson with much devotion, and I preached two short sermons, which he heard with great affection. He went into his chamber about midnight, and I stayed the whole night in the adjoining room. He went to bed about two in the morning, and was fast asleep about four, when, by his desire, we called him. He was quickly dressed, and lost no time in shaving, for he said he was not concerned in his good looks that day. He went two or three times back into his chamber to pray by himself, and then came and prayed again with Tillotson and me. He drank a little tea and some sherry, and then he said now he had done with time, and was going to eternity. He asked what he should give the executioner, and I told him ten guineas; he smiled, and said it was a pretty thing to give a fee to have his head cut off. The Sheriffs came about ten o'clock; Lord Cavendish was waiting below to take leave of him. They embraced very tenderly. Lord Russell on a second thought came back and pressed Cavendish earnestly to apply himself more to religion, telling him what great comfort and support he felt from it now in his extremity. Tillotson and I went in the coach with him. Some of the crowd wept, while others insulted him; he was touched with the one expression, but did not seem provoked by the other. He was singing psalms most of the way, and said he hoped to sing better soon. Looking at the great crowd he said 'I hope I shall soon see a much better assembly.' He walked about the scaffold four or five times, then he turned to the Sheriffs, and in presenting the paper he protested his innocence of any design against the King's life, or any attempt to subvert the Government. He prayed God to preserve the Protestant religion, and earnestly wished that Protestants should love one another, and not make way for Popery by their animosities. He forgave all his enemies, and died in charity with all mankind. After this he prayed again with Archbishop Tillotson, and more than once by himself. Then William Russell stood erect, arranged his dress, and, without the slightest change of countenance, laid his noble head upon the block, 'which was struck off (says Evelyn) by three butcherly strokes.'

Five years afterwards when James the Second stood on the brink of ruin, he did not disdain to apply to the Earl of Bedford for help. 'My Lord,' he said, 'you are an honest man, and of great credit in the country, and can do me signal service.' 'Ah, sire,' replied the Earl, 'I am old and feeble, and can be of little use, but I once had a son who could have assisted you, and he is no more.' By which answer James was so struck, that he could not speak for several moments.

No. 14.   WILLIAM HARVEY, M.D.
Black gown.   Black skull-cap.
BORN 1578, DIED 1657-8.
By RILEY.

SON of Thomas Harvey of Folkestone, in Kent, by Joan Hawke, and eldest of seven sons and two daughters. The parents were well-to-do people, who brought up their children carefully and respectably. Mrs. Harvey seems to have been a most estimable woman, if we only believe one half the virtues ascribed to her on the tablet in Folkestone Church, where she lies buried; the epitaph, though couched in the eulogistic and lengthy style which was the fashion of the day, is sufficiently characteristic to merit insertion. The mother of a great man is in our eyes always deserving of notice.

'She was a godly, harmless woman, a chaste, loving wife, a charitable, quiet neighbour, a comfortable and friendly matron, a provident housewife and tender mother. Elected of God, may her soul rest in heaven (as her body in this grave), to her a happy advantage, to hers an unhappy loss.'

When only ten years old William Harvey went to a Grammar School, and subsequently to Caius College, Cambridge, where, we are told, 'he studied classics, dialectics, and physics.' It was the fashion of the day for young men of any standing to finish their education on the Continent, in one or other of those schools of learning and science which were indeed the resort of the youth of all nations. Harvey fixed his choice on Padua, then especially rich in eminent Professors in all branches of learning. He had been early destined, both by the wishes of his family and his own inclination, for the medical profession; and at Padua, under the auspices of the celebrated Fabricius of Acquapendente and others, our young Englishman, whose zeal was equal to his intelligence, laid the foundation of his future greatness, and made rapid strides in the path of fame. He remained five years at Padua, and before his departure, at the age of twenty-four, received his doctor's diploma, with 'licence to practise in every land and seat of learning.' On his return to England he obtained his doctor's degree at his old University of Cambridge, after which he settled in London, and married the daughter of one Lancelot Brown, M.D. Harvey soon got into extensive practice, enlarged his connection daily, and, while rising step by step in his profession, made himself beloved (as is mostly the case with the true disciple of St. Luke) by the skill and charity he exercised among the poor and afflicted by whom he was surrounded.

Before long he was elected a member of St. Bartholomew's Hospital, and subsequently Principal Physician of that important establishment, where, in the course of his tenure, he introduced the most stringent reforms and regulations, which were considered needlessly severe by the younger students, who had grown into habits of laxity and idleness. But neither the duties of his office, nor his practice which he carried on outside the walls, were allowed to interfere in any way with his literary labours. Making the profoundest researches into every branch of medical science, perusing and weighing the arguments of those very writers whom he was destined to eclipse; he attracted the notice of King James the First, one of whose redeeming qualities it was to encourage learning, and who found great delight in the society of eminent men. The King named Harvey Physician Extraordinary, with a reversionary promise of the regular post at Court when it should become vacant, which did not occur till after the accession of Charles the First. He was also body physician to several noblemen and gentlemen of eminence, such as the Lord Chancellor Bacon and Thomas Howard, Earl of Arundel, with whom he travelled on the Continent. He was appointed Lecturer to the Royal College of Physicians, in Amen Corner, where, with some interruptions (through absence, Court duties, and other hindrances), he continued for many years to attract and interest his colleagues by his knowledge and eloquence. It was in the course of these lectures that he first promulgated his wondrous doctrines on the motions of the heart and the circulation of the blood; a subject with which the name of William Harvey is indissolubly connected. The theories that had been hatching in his prolific mind for long now took form and shape in his immortal work, which he dedicated to King Charles, and to his own College. It was this work (although one of many) which enriched the science of medicine, and rendered his name immortal. The circulation of the blood had from time immemorial been the theme of dispute and discussion among men of all nations; but it was reserved, says Birch, for William Harvey in 1628 to publish a book which was the clearest, the shortest, and the most convincing that had ever yet been written on the subject. The startling discoveries, and the bold manner in which they were expounded, kindled a flame of antagonism and rivalry in the medical world. Learned Professors, and men who professed without learning, rose to denounce, to question, to deny him even the merit of originality, for had not the same theories been known to the ancients? To the manifold attacks by which he was assailed Harvey maintained for the most part a dignified silence, though compelled in some cases to rise up and defend himself and his opinions from adversaries, both English and foreign.

In 1636 he accompanied his friend and patron, Thomas Howard, Earl of Arundel, when that nobleman went on a special mission to the Emperor of Germany. Harvey did not neglect this opportunity of making the acquaintance of all the eminent men of science in the country, who in their turn were desirous (from mingled motives) of meeting a man with whose name Europe was now ringing. In a conclave of medical men at Nürnberg our doctor made a public declaration of his professional faith, when he was met by the most strenuous opposition. The learned Caspar Hoffman, in particular, was so violent and unreasonable in his arguments, that William Harvey, after listening with singular forbearance for a considerable time, laid down the scalpel, which he held and quietly left the apartment. It was in this expedition with Lord Arundel that one of his Excellency's gentlemen told Aubrey that Lord Arundel was rendered very anxious by the frequent explorings of his physician into the woods, where was great fear, not only of wild beasts, but also of thieves, and where, indeed, the doctor one time narrowly escaped with life. But Harvey would not neglect the chance of studying the strange trees and foreign plants, and adding to his collection of toads, frogs, and the like, for the purpose of experimenting upon them—was sometimes like to be lost indeed, so that my Lord Ambassador was angry with him. With all these contentions and animadversions we are not surprised to hear that at one time Harvey's practice declined, and Aubrey says, 'He was treated by many as a visionary and a madman, and though everybody admired his anatomy, most people questioned his therapeutics, so much so that his bills (*i.e.* recipes and prescriptions) were not worth threepence.' He now gave himself up to the prosecution of his Court duties, and was indefatigable in his attendance on the King. The relationship between Charles and his physician was of the most friendly and intimate nature. Harvey speaks of his royal master in terms of true affection, while the King took great delight in frequenting the doctor's dissecting-room, and studying anatomy and medicine under his tutelage. On the breaking out of the civil wars Harvey became more than ever attached in every sense of the word to the person of the King, following him wheresoever he went, to court and camp. On their return from Scotland our peace-loving doctor was present at the battle of Edgehill, where Aubrey records a very characteristic, and almost comical adventure. It was in 1642, during the fight in question, that Harvey was intrusted with the care of the Prince of Wales and the Duke of York. He accordingly withdrew with his young charges to what he considered the shelter of a hedge, and finding the time hang heavy on his hands, he took a book from his pocket, which he began calmly and leisurely to peruse, when a large bullet grazed and disturbed the grass at his feet, and induced him to move further from the heat of the battle. Again we quote Aubrey, who met him at Oxford, where the Court then was, and though 'too young to become acquainted with so learned a doctor,' yet he remembers well how Harvey would come to our College to the chambers of George Bathurst, tutor, who kept hens for the hatching purposes in his rooms. Harvey would break the eggs daily at intervals in order to watch the different progress of formation towards the 'perfect chick';

and all this with a view to the medical works he was writing. How widely at variance were these calm studies compared with the wild turmoil of political and military excitement by which he was surrounded! The Wardenship of Merton College becoming vacant by the resignation of Sir Matthew Brent, a Parliamentarian, the King recommended Harvey for the vacant post, which he obtained, but did not enjoy long, for when Oxford surrendered to the Roundheads, Brent resumed his office. We cannot be surprised to hear that so loyal a subject as Harvey incurred the ire of Cromwell, and on the doctor's return to London he found his house sacked, the furniture destroyed, and, worse than all, as he himself told Aubrey, 'No griefe was so crucifyinge as the loss of those papers (treating of his medical experiences and experiments) which neither love nor money could replace.' It must have been about the year 1646 that Dr. Harvey made up his mind to resign his place at Court. Many reasons were given for this step, many apologies made for his forsaking his royal master; but he was near upon seventy, and it appears natural that a man of so peaceful a nature and of such studious taste should prefer a calmer existence than that of 'following the drum.' His retirement not only enabled him to pursue the bent of his inclinations and to indulge in contemplation, but also to enjoy the society of his brothers, who were of that number that verily dwelt together in unity. They held their elder in honour and affection, and vied with each other in welcoming him warmly to their respective homes. His next brother Eliab seems to have been his favourite, as he made his home for the most part either at the said Eliab's London residence of Cokaine House, near the Poultry, or at Roehampton, in Surrey. On the leads of the former dwelling the doctor was wont to pass many hours in contemplation, arranging his different stations with a view to the sun and wind. At Combe there were caverns specially constructed in the garden for the physician to meditate, as he always found darkness most conducive to thought. The thrifty Eliab took William's financial affairs in hand, which he conducted with so much energy and discernment as to increase his brother's income, and enable him to indulge his generous propensities towards private individuals and public institutions. He became a munificent benefactor to his beloved College of Physicians, both by gifts in his lifetime, and bequest by testament. He enlarged the buildings, added a wing, and a large hall for conference, endowed it with a library and a museum, and, in fact, was so noble in his gifts that the grateful College erected a statue in his honour, with a long and flattering inscription. But, alas! all these valuable additions, together with the whole edifice, were destroyed in the Great Fire of London. At the age of seventy-one the doctor's energy remained so unabated, that not only did he continue his literary labours, but he travelled to Italy with his friend and disciple Sir George Brent. On the last day of June 1657 William Harvey was stricken with the palsy, and, on endeavouring to speak, found that he had lost the power to do so. He ordered his apothecary by signs to 'lett him blood,' but this gave him no relief, and his professional knowledge warned him that the end was approaching. He therefore sent for his brother and nephews, to whom he himself delivered some little token of affection, a watch or what not, bidding them tenderly farewell, with dumb but eloquent signs of affection. He died the same day as he was stricken. His friend Aubrey exonerates him from the false charge of having hastened his own death by drinking opium, which he occasionally used as an alleviation of pain, but said Harvey had 'an easy passport.'

A long train of his colleagues from the Royal College attended his funeral, and Aubrey himself was one of the bearers. He was buried at Hempstead, in Essex, and was 'lapped' in a leaden case, which was shaped in form of the body, with a label bearing the illustrious name of William Harvey, M.D., on his breast.

The last will and testament of men who lay claim to any celebrity appear to us to merit notice as indicative of character. Harvey's will did not in any way belie his life. He left his faithful steward and brother, Eliab Harvey, the bulk of his property in money and land, as likewise (Aubrey thinks out of tender sentiment) his silver coffee-pot; for the brothers were wont to drink coffee together at a time when it was reckoned an uncommon luxury, before coffee-houses were prevalent in England. To all his other relations he left small sums that they might purchase remembrances; to his College, and to more than one hospital, generous bequests; scarcely any one was forgotten. To his dear and learned friend Mr. Thomas Hobbes £10, to Dr. Scarborough his velvet embroidered gown, to another his case of silver-mounted surgical instruments, and so on. Nor were his faithful servants, who had tended him in sickness, forgotten; 'the pretty young wench' who waited on him at Oxford, and to whom Aubrey alludes in jesting terms, in spite of Harvey's proverbial insensibility to female charms, proved a most tender nurse, and was gratefully remembered. We hear very little at any time about Mistress Harvey, or the esteem in which her husband held her, but we are told she had a parrot, whose prattle much amused the learned doctor.

He corresponded with learned men, both at home and abroad, and was linked in friendship with such men as Hobbes, Robert Boyle, Cowley, and the like. By nature he was hot-tempered and outspoken, although a courtier. He rode to visit his patients on horseback, with a servant to follow him on foot—'a decent custom,' Aubrey thinks, the discontinuance of which he regrets. The same authority says Harvey 'was of the lowest stature, and an olivaster complexion, like unto wainscott; little eye, round, bright, and black, and hair like the raven, but quite white before his death,' which could scarcely be wondered at, as he was then eighty years of age. His friend, the learned Mr. Hobbes, says that Harvey was 'the only man, perhaps, who ever lived to see his own doctrines established in his lifetime.' This statement, the truth of which appears more than questionable, it is easy to imagine, was put forth under the influence of mortified feeling on the part of the 'philosopher of Malmesbury.' We refer the reader who is curious in such research to the catalogues of the principal scientific libraries, both in England and on the Continent, for a list of this great physician's professional works, as their names alone would enlarge in an inconvenient manner the bulk of our volume.

No. 15. THE HONOURABLE EDWARD RUSSELL.

In armour. Red sash over right shoulder. White collar, with tassels. Long hair.

DIED 1665.

BY REMÉE.

E was the youngest son of Francis, fourth Earl of Bedford, by Catherine Brydges. He married Penelope, daughter and co-heir of Sir Moses Hill of Hillsborough Castle, Ireland (Knight Marshal of Ulster, and ancestor of the present Marquis of Downshire), and widow of Sir William Brooke, Knight, by whom he had five sons and daughters. His second son was eventually raised to the Peerage by the title of the Earl of Oxford. Edward Russell survived his wife, and, dying in 1665, was buried at Chenies.

No. 16.

WILLIAM RUSSELL, FIFTH EARL, FIRST DUKE OF BEDFORD.

In armour. Lace cravat. Wig.

BORN 1613, DIED 1700.

BY SIR GODFREY KNELLER.

E was the eldest son of Francis Russell, fourth Earl of Bedford, by Catherine Brydges, daughter and co-heir of Lord Chandos. He was educated at Magdalen College, Oxford; and after travelling abroad for two years, we are told he returned home in 1634, a very handsome and accomplished gentleman. Of his personal beauty and noble bearing the fine portrait of William Russell, and Lord Digby, by Vandyck, bears undoubted testimony. He had been created Knight of the Bath at the coronation of Charles the First. The representative of a high-born family, and heir to a very large fortune, young Lord Russell was keenly watched by the match-makers of the day. At that time three rival beauties divided the admiration of the Court—Lady Elizabeth Cecil, Lady Dorothy Sidney, and Lady Anne Carr, the only child of the Earl and Countess of Somerset. She was born in the Tower at the time of her mother's imprisonment for the murder of Sir Thomas Overbury, and had been brought up in total ignorance of her parents' ignominy. 'The voice goes,' says a contemporary writer, 'that young Russell bends somewhat towards the Lady Anne Carr.' One would not be surprised to hear that Lord Bedford was most adverse to the union. He trembled for the future welfare of his son, and the honour of his house, for heavy was the blot on the young lady's 'scutcheon. He promised his consent to any other union his son should project; but it was too late: Lord Russell's choice was free no more, and the sequel proved the selection had been for his own happiness, and that of the whole family. The King interested himself in the cause of the young lovers, and sent the Duke of Lennox to mediate with Lord Bedford in the matter. Lord Somerset, with all his crimes on his head, had proved himself the most tender and devoted of fathers, giving his child an excellent and strictly virtuous education, and he made every sacrifice in his power to give her a good dowry, seeing that her poverty was an additional obstacle to the marriage in Lord Bedford's eyes; so Somerset sold his house at Chiswick, his furniture, his plate and jewels; in fact denuded himself of almost all he had, to make settlements on Lady Anne, 'for,' said he to the Lord Chamberlain, 'if one of us is to be undone by the marriage, let it be myself, rather than my own deserving child.' And so came about this marriage, and the lovely creature, whose sweet innocent young face is familiar to all lovers of Vandyck, became the wife of Lord Russell, and the future mother of the patriot William.

Lord Russell sat in Parliament for Tavistock, having for colleague the famous Mr. Pym; but in the commencement of his career he did not take much part in debate, but was chiefly employed in carrying messages from the Lower to the Upper House.

The death of Francis, fourth Earl of Bedford, caused great excitement in political circles, and the new Earl received a deputation from the House of Peers expressive of condolence, and the hope that 'as soon as his Lordship's sorrow would allow him, he would take his seat, for no one could better supply the place of his deceased father.' These conjectures were confirmed, for the new Lord followed in the footsteps of his father, and in all the part he took in the coming struggles, he was ever ready to support liberal and enlightened views, and to advocate what he considered necessary reforms; withstanding undue encroachments on the part of the King. He was, however, inclined to wise and moderate views from the beginning, and deeply regretted the circumstances which had led to civil dissension and open war; but the times were too stormy, and the pressure of the political barometer too high, to allow of a middle course. Disgusted with what he considered the arbitrary measures and the obstinacy of the King, Lord Bedford now espoused the cause of the Parliament, and even accepted the post of General in their army. He besieged the Royalist forces in Sherborne Castle, and afterwards, on joining the Earl of Essex on the eve of the battle of Edgehill, he accepted, under that general, the command of the *corps de reserve*. His conduct in the action gained him great distinction, as it was supposed to be owing to his skill and courage that the defeat of the Parliamentarians was averted, 'for Lord Bedford brought up very gallantly amidst a play of cannon.' He was ever ready to propose and to facilitate every means of pacification between Charles and his people, but all these endeavours proving fruitless, and finding himself in opposition to the *ultra* opinions and measures of the Roundheads, he, with some other Lords, determined on joining the King at Oxford. One of his biographers says, the Earl of Bedford came to Oxford, had his introduction, made a declaration of the motives which had actuated his past conduct, and received a formal pardon under the Great Seal. The King was naturally inclined to welcome so noble an adherent, but was rather lukewarm in his manner, while the Queen and the greater part of the courtiers treated him with much discourtesy. He fought with the Royalists at the siege of Gloucester and the battle of Newbury, where the gallant Falkland was killed. The Parliament, infuriated at Lord Bedford's secession, sequestrated his estates; but this sentence was reversed shortly after the battle of Marston Moor in 1644.

Entrance Hall.

The next year Lord Bedford, with Lord Carlisle and four other Peers, who had come from the King's quarters, went to the House of Parliament and took the Covenant before the Commissioners of the Great Seal; this being the only compliance made by Lord Bedford with the faction he had abandoned. He now retired from public life, absented himself from Parliament, and sought that quiet and domestic peace in the bosom of his family, for which it may be well imagined he had often sighed amid the turmoil and strife of political and military life. He repaired to his home at Woburn Abbey, where, between the years 1645 and 1647, his royal master visited him on three separate occasions. After the execution of the King, and during the vicissitudes of the Commonwealth and the Protectorate, Lord Bedford continued to live in seclusion, and it was not until the Restoration (to which event he contributed, as far as in him lay, both by his influence and his aid in pecuniary matters) that he reappeared in public. How ill was he repaid by an ungrateful and cruel King! Lord Bedford carried St. Edward's sceptre at the coronation of Charles the Second, and some time after received the Blue Ribbon of the Garter. He belonged to a large number of loyal spirits, who, after assisting and rejoicing in the return of the lawful Sovereign, experienced the most bitter disappointment at the tyrannical and unconstitutional course pursued by Charles, and following in the steps of his father, stood up manfully against the encroachments on civil and religious liberty; conduct which was supported and nobly carried out in the House of Commons by his son William, Lord Russell, whose union with Lady Vaughan about 1669 (better known to history as Rachel, Lady Russell) was a source of unalloyed satisfaction to Lord and Lady Bedford, to whom she became a tender and devoted daughter. In the life of William, Lord Russell, we have given full details of his political career, of the animosity his independent line of conduct aroused in the minds of the King and the Duke of York, of his arrest on the false pretence of being implicated in the Rye House Plot, of his unjust trial and hurried execution, particulars of which it would be superfluous to repeat here. Lady Russell spent the early days of her widowhood, and indeed the greater part of her subsequent life, at Woburn, with her father-in-law, affording and imparting sympathy. Lord Russell's execution took place in July 1683, and within a year his fond mother followed him to the grave. Since the death of that beloved son, Lady Bedford's health had gradually declined; she pined away silently, almost imperceptibly; but there is little doubt her death was accelerated by a strange and unforeseen incident. She was sitting one day in the gallery at Woburn, when her attention was attracted by a pamphlet which contained the whole history of her mother's life, her marriage and divorce from Lord Essex, and the tragedy connected with the murder of Sir Thomas Overbury, together with the complicity of both parents—the mother, whose memory she knew no reason to despise, the father whom she fondly believed she had every reason to adore. The next person who entered the room found the unhappy woman senseless on the floor, the fatal book beside her. It appears from some letters of her daughter-in-law at the time, that the family not only believed that this sad incident had hastened her death, but that if her life had been spared, her reason would have been endangered.

The remainder of Lord Bedford's life is so intimately bound up with that of his daughter-in-law and her children, that we must refer the reader to our notice of Lady Russell for further particulars, even the passage in which we have given the account of the creation of the Dukedom, which honour was doubly acceptable to the aged Duke, as a tribute to the memory of his lamented son. His love for his grandchildren, and the tender letters he writes to their mother on their account, his delight in the society of Mistress Katey, his little playfellow of nine years old, when he was past eighty, all vouch for the gentleness of heart which characterised the first Duke of Bedford. He had lived to see his son's memory vindicated, his son's widow honoured and sought after by every class in the kingdom, beginning with the Sovereigns, William and Mary; the attainder reversed, his grandchildren prosperous, his grandson and heir married with his sanction and approbation, and the family name, in which he had a right to glory, respected through the kingdom. He was ready to depart, and 'now his daily prayer was to the effect that the God in whom he had so humbly and faithfully trusted would grant him an easy passage to the tomb.' And never did any person leave this world with greater inward peace, or with less struggle and discomposure; his lamp of life was not blown out: the oil wasted by degrees, nature was spent, and he fell asleep on the 7th September 1700, aged eighty-seven. He was buried at Chenies by the side of his beloved wife.

No. 17. SIR THOMAS MYDDLETON, BART., OF CHIRK.

Brown dress. Purple sleeves. Lace cravat. Long hair.

DIED 1683.

BY RUSSELL.

E was the son of Sir Thomas Myddleton, first Baronet, who began his military career as a Parliamentarian, afterwards became a zealous adherent of the Royal cause, and was created a Baronet in 1660. The subject of the present notice married, first, Elizabeth, daughter and co-heir of Sir Thomas Wilbraham of Woodney; and, secondly, Charlotte, daughter of Sir Orlando

Bridgeman, Bart.; and had an only daughter, Charlotte, married first to Edward, Earl of Warwick, and secondly to the Right Hon. Joseph Addison.

No. 18.   THE HONOURABLE FRANCIS RUSSELL.

In armour.   Long fair hair.

DIED 1641.

BY REMÉE.

E was the second son of Francis, fourth Earl of Bedford, by Catherine Brydges. He married Catherine, daughter of Lord Grey de Wark, and widow of Sir Edward Moseley, Bart., and of the Lord North and Gray, by whom he had no children. Francis Russell died in France shortly before his father. He was brother to the first Countess of Bradford, of the Newport family.

BREAKFAST-ROOM.

K

BREAKFAST-ROOM.

No. 1. PRINCE MAURICE.

As a boy. In the character of Cupid.

BORN 1620, DIED 1653.

BY HONTHORST.

E was the fourth son of Frederic, Elector Palatine (King of Bohemia), by Elizabeth, Princess of England, daughter of James the First. After the battle of Prague, which wrecked their fortunes, the unhappy ex-King and Queen were driven from their palace at Prague, compelled to fly for their lives by unfrequented roads, and through the blinding snowstorms, which impeded the progress of their coach, and from which the fugitives were obliged to alight, and take horse.

Elizabeth displayed the utmost courage and fortitude, despite the intensity of the weather and the delicacy of her health, and mounted gladly on a pillion behind a young English volunteer of the name of Hopton, who would often speak in after-days with love and veneration of his royal fellow-traveller, the Queen of Hearts, the only sovereignty that was now left her. In their distress the unhappy pair sought about for some place of shelter where Elizabeth might be cared for in her hour of approaching trial and her husband appealed to his brother-in-law, George William of Brandenburg, for the loan of one of his castles, either of Spandau or Custrine. The answer was a grudging permission to inhabit the latter residence, although the owner assured Frederic it was no place for a Queen just fresh from a palace; that it was not commodious or safe from the incursions of their enemies; and, moreover, they would be exposed to cold and famine, as there was no fuel and no food. The fugitives found this account but too true, and even this surly permission would have been withheld but for the intercession of the British Envoy, Wotton. Moreover, their parsimonious host bargained with his needy relatives to defray all expenses, but Elizabeth's condition allowed of no alternative. Three days after their arrival Prince Maurice was born in this dreary old barrack, with its bare walls and unfurnished interior—a strange contrast to the scene of splendour and festivity which characterised the birth of his brother Rupert. Before the proper time had elapsed that it was advisable for her to travel, the ex-Queen was hurried away, accompanied by little Rupert, to Wolfenbüttel, and afterwards to the Hague, where she found a generous protector and devoted friend in the Stadtholder; the new-born infant being despatched to the care of his widowed grandmother, the Electress Juliana, in Polish Russia. Poor child! he had not the traditional good fortune of one born on Christmas Day. From his earliest childhood he bore his brother Rupert the most devoted affection, and through their lives they were brothers in very truth—brothers in arms and affection; their paths strangely intertwined for soldiers of fortune; they were both prematurely brave, and early initiated into the profession they so much adorned. When together at the siege of Breda, Maurice, waking in the night, heard a noise for which he could not account, so he roused Rupert, and they crept out together in the dark, and were just in time to save the garrison from a surprise. In 1638 Prince Maurice prosecuted his studies at a French University, and in 1642 gained permission to accompany Rupert, who had been appointed to a high command in the army of their uncle, Charles the First. This gallant pair vied with each other in loyalty and devotion to the English King. Their bravery, their exploits, the various commands they filled, the numerous actions in which they fought (frequently side by side), all these incidents belong to the chronicles of the civil wars of the period. In 1646 the brothers left England, Prince Rupert proceeding to St. Germain to join the Queen-mother there in exile, while Prince Maurice embarked for Holland. The subsequent life of this Prince appears to have been almost entirely passed on the decks of the varied vessels which he in turn commanded, for both he and Rupert secured glory and renown on the broad ocean, as they had already done in the battle-field, and their voyages were frequently made in company. In the notice of the elder, we have given the account of a touching episode in the lives of the two brothers, which we therefore omit here. But Maurice was doomed to find a watery grave in the year 1653, in a hurricane which overtook his vessel off the Virgin Islands. The following is a description of the tragic event: 'In this fatal wreck, besides many great gentlemen and others, the sea, to glut itself, swallowed the Prince, whose fame the mouth of detraction cannot blast. His very enemies bewailed his loss. Many had more power, few more merit; he lived beloved, and died bewailed.' Two years after his death there was a rumour that he still lived (but the false report soon died away), that he had been captured by a pirate, and was a slave in Africa, but this unlikely tale gained little or no credence.

No. 8.   COLONEL WEST.

Black cloak over doublet of same colour. Left hand gloved with white glove and holding the other. Large white cuffs turned back. Hand resting on hip. White deep turned-down collar with tassels.

By WALKER.

E was a distinguished Parliamentarian officer, and much valued by Cromwell. He was engaged in Inverkeithing fight in 1651, and was commended in Oliver Cromwell's letter to the Speaker of the Parliament of England, reporting the result of that engagement, which he described as an 'unspeakable mercy.'

No. 16.

THOMAS WRIOTHESLEY, EARL OF SOUTHAMPTON.

Robes of the Garter. Wand of office.

DIED 1667.

By SIR PETER LELY.

E was the second born but only surviving son of the third Earl, by Elizabeth, daughter of John Vernon of Hodnet, County Salop. Educated at Eton and Oxford, where he distinguished himself, and afterwards travelled abroad; remained some time in France, where he probably espoused his first wife, and afterwards proceeded to the Low Countries. His father and elder brother had also gone thither, and were attacked by fever.

The youth died, and his father (travelling before it was prudent for him to do so), borne down by sorrow, soon followed his beloved child to the grave. Thomas, who had now become Earl of Southampton, found on his return to England that public affairs were in great confusion. The Parliamentarians did all in their power to gain over the young nobleman to their side, but he disapproved of their proceedings, and would take no part in them. He was soon after appointed Privy Councillor and Lord of the Bedchamber to the King, and became henceforth, in every sense of the word, attached to the royal person, to whom he was an excellent friend, often giving him unpalatable advice. He used to sleep in the King's apartment, and to the best of his power soothed his hours of mental anguish. In 1647, when the unhappy monarch fled from Hampton Court, he took shelter at Titchfield, in Hampshire, Lord Southampton's country-house, and when brought back to the palace in the hands of his enemies, his first request was for the attendance of his trusty friend. This permission was granted him, and Southampton was one of the last allowed to remain with his royal master, and one of the four mourners who paid the last sad duties to his remains. With Charles the Second he kept up a continued correspondence, and supplied the exile with large sums, hastening to meet him on his arrival in England, when he was rewarded by being made Knight of the Garter, as were other faithful adherents to the Crown, and was shortly afterwards appointed Lord High Treasurer. In this capacity he showed so much independence of spirit and interest in the public welfare as to offend the King, who did not, however, remove him from his office, which was exercised by Southampton, although suffering from a terrible and painful disease which made business occasionally irksome to him. To his credit be it spoken, that during seven years' management of the Treasury he made but an ordinary fortune, disdaining to sell places, as many of his predecessors had done.

The Earl of Southampton was thrice married: first, to Rachel, daughter of Daniel de Ruvigny, in France, by whom he had two sons, who died young, and three daughters, the second of whom was Rachel, the faithful wife and widow of the patriot, William, Lord Russell; his second Countess was Elizabeth, daughter and co-heir of Francis Booth, Lord Dunsmore, by whom he had four girls; and his third wife was the daughter of William, second Duke of Somerset, and widow of Viscount Molyneux. He died at Southampton House, in Bloomsbury, which he bequeathed to his daughter, Lady Russell, and was buried at Titchfield. By his death the title of Southampton in the Wriothesley family became extinct.

No. 28. COLONEL, AFTERWARDS LORD GORING.

Slashed doublet. Long fair hair.

DIED 1662 *v.p.*

BY STONE AFTER VANDYCK.

SIR GEORGE GORING of Hurstpierpoint, County Sussex, was created in 1629 Baron Goring, and in 1645 Earl of Norwich. He married Mary, daughter of Edward Neville, Lord Abergavenny. Their third eldest son was George, the subject of this notice, who distinguished himself greatly in the civil wars. He married in early life Lady Lettice Boyle, daughter of the Earl of Cork. He was wild, eccentric, and extravagant, and Lord Wentworth (afterwards Earl of Strafford), speaking of him in a letter to Lord Carlisle, 1633, says: 'Young Mr. Goring is gone to travel, having run himself out of £8000, which he purposes to redeem by frugality abroad, unless my Lord Cork can be induced to put to his helping hand, which I have undertaken to solicit for him the best I can, and shall do it with all the power and care my credit and wit shall in any way suggest unto me.' The noble writer was successful in his negotiation, and Lord Cork was most generous and liberal on this and several other occasions to a son-in-law who gave him much trouble. Not long after the marriage Lord Cork thus writes, in speaking of George Goring : ' After borrowing money from me for himself and his father, he departed from us without once taking leave of me, and leaving his wife and servants, posted through Scotland on to England on the choice gray gelding I bestowed upon him called Gray Brown, hath much disquieted me, his wife, and friends.' His poor wife had good reason to be disquieted on this and many other occasions, but she seems to have retained a real affection for her unworthy husband, willing to join him at any summons, and frequently interceding with her generous father for so-called loans and large sums, which never appear to have been repaid.

George Goring, on his arrival in the Low Countries, enlisted as a soldier, entered Lord Vere's regiment, and soon gained a high command, distinguishing himself at the siege of Breda. On his return to England he was made Governor of Portsmouth, in which capacity he got into trouble with the Parliament, and was summoned before the House of Commons on suspicion of favouring the Royal cause. Anxious to provide for his own interests by pleasing both sides, he contrived to give satisfaction to the Parliament, and was therefore exonerated. Goring was indeed anything but straightforward in his dealings; Lord Clarendon says of him : ' He could help himself with all the intimation of doubt, or fear, or shame, or simplicity in his face that might gain belief to a greater degree than I ever saw in any man, and could seem most confounded when he was best resolved, and to want words when they flowed from no man with greater power.' He cajoled the popular party, corresponded secretly with the King in 1642, threw off the mask he had worn as adherent to the Parliament, and declared openly that he held Portsmouth for Charles the First. The town was besieged by sea and land, and surrendered after a meagre defence; Goring stipulating that he might be allowed to transport himself beyond the seas, which caused great astonishment, as also did his appointment (on his return in 1644) to the command of cavalry in the Royal army in Lincolnshire. He now continued to distinguish himself greatly in the service of the King, and was present in almost every action. In 1646, his father being created Earl of Norwich, he became Lord Goring, and held the commission of Lieutenant-General of several counties, in which capacity he did little good, setting a bad example to the troops by his irregular and immoral conduct. Clarendon says of him that he had a good understanding, a sharp wit, and keen courage, but he did not value his promise or friendship according to any rules of honour or integrity. 'He loved no man so well but he would cozen him and expose him to ridicule.' The same historian speaks of Goring's immoderate ambition, dissimulation, and want of religion. He continued his vacillating line of conduct, and when in difficulties pleaded illness, and gained permission to go to Bath for a cure, but returned to active service, became a Privy Councillor, and had undeserved favours showered upon him by the King. His whole career was marked by contrasts of success and failure, courage and blundering, and animosity towards those who like Prince Rupert filled a high position, and stood well in the opinion of others. After many vicissitudes he resolved to leave England, and proceeded to the Netherlands, where he became Lieutenant-General of the Spanish army, and afterwards

Breakfast-Room. 83

obtained the same command in Spain under Don John de Silva, who, finding that he was in communication with Cardinal Mazarin, had him seized at the head of his troops, and sent prisoner to Madrid. Writers differ as to the termination of this eccentric man's career. Some say he was put to death in prison for treason, and others that he entered a monastery and died in the habit of a Dominican friar.

Lord Goring had no children. Dying in the lifetime of his father, Lord Norwich was succeeded by his second son, Charles, who married Alice, daughter of Robert Leman, Esq., and widow of Sir Richard Baker, Knight, but having no children the titles of Norwich and Goring became extinct.

No. 30.   PRINCE RUPERT.

In a classical dress, as Mars.

BORN 1619, DIED 1682.

BY HONTHORST.

E was the third son of Frederic, Elector Palatine, and King of Bohemia, by Princess Elizabeth of England, daughter of James the First. Born at Prague during the short-lived period of his parents' prosperity, while inhabiting the Palace of the Bohemian capital. More than half a century had elapsed since the birth of a royal Prince at Prague, and the event was the occasion of great excitement and rejoicing. Persons of all classes were invited to have a glimpse of the royal infant, swathed in rich wrappings of gold and embroidery. Nobles and ladies, burghers and their wives, officers of state, soldiers, peasants, all flocked to the Palace, and clustered

round the cradle of the future hero. His father thought well to name him Rupert, after the wise and fortunate Elector who, on the death of Wenceslaus, ascended the Imperial throne: and the ceremony of baptism was conducted on a scale of great magnificence, which helped not a little to drain the ill-filled coffers of Frederic and Elizabeth. On the other hand, donations of all kinds poured in from the nobles, the burghers, and their respective wives. Contributions of fruit and flowers were presented by the poorer population, offerings which were most graciously received by the gentle-hearted mother.

Her two elder sons were respectively heirs to titles (alas! how empty) of King, and Elector Palatine. The Bohemian Ministry, willing to do honour to a Prince born 'in their midst,' bestowed on the new-born babe the dignity of Duke of Lithuania, which the child did not long enjoy, seeing that a few months after his birth the decisive battle of Prague was the means of driving his parents from their newly-acquired kingdom, penniless and homeless wanderers, compelled to solicit shelter and assistance from cold relatives and fickle friends.

Rupert was the only one of her children who accompanied Elizabeth on her miserable flight from Custrin to Holland (a circumstance to which we have alluded in the sketch of his brother Maurice), where the ex-Queen with her family resided for many years, and where five children were born to her. Little Rupert was sent to the College at Leyden, where his eldest brother Henry was a student, and had already distinguished himself greatly. Amongst other accomplishments, Henry was an elegant letter-writer, and kept up a frequent correspondence with his mother. In one of his letters he tells how 'dear Rupert is a most lively boy,' and amused the students when he first arrived by speaking to them in Bohemian.

A soldier at heart from his earliest childhood, Rupert did not remain long at Leyden, but entered the army under Henry Frederic of Nassau, and (Lodge tells us) was present at the siege of Thynberg, although another biographer places the date of his first action several years later. Be this as it may, in 1637 he marched with his brother, Charles Louis, who now called himself Elector Palatine (their father being dead), against the Imperialists. The gallant Lord Craven had constituted himself the guardian of 'the Palatine Princes,' and accompanied them in the expedition, writing frequently to their mother at the Hague, to give tidings of Charles and the beloved Rupert. Lord Craven had warmly espoused the cause of Frederic, and was now the devoted friend of the royal widow and her family. He and his two charges distinguished themselves during the siege of Lippe, but being worsted in an encounter with General Hatzfeldt, Charles Louis had a narrow escape of his life. He crossed the river in his coach, and, clinging to the shrubs and underwood, climbed up on the precipitous bank of the opposite shore, and made his way to Holland. His brother and Lord Craven were both taken prisoners by the Imperialists, and carried to Vienna, where they were lodged in the castle. With much difficulty Rupert found means to have a few lines conveyed to his mother, wherein, after some tender expressions of filial love and respect, he assured her that no power on earth should induce him to renounce his party, or abjure his faith. Lord Craven succeeded in regaining his freedom, by paying the large ransom of £20,000; but all attempts to procure the deliverance of Rupert proved unavailing. It was only at the expiration of three years, and on condition that he would undertake never again to bear arms against the Emperor, that the young Prince was set at liberty, shortly after which event he received an offer from his uncle, Charles the First, of the command of the cavalry in the

Royal army, the King having unfurled his standard against the Parliamentarians. He was accompanied by his brother Maurice, whose love and admiration for his elder were unbounded; and the exploits of these gallant Princes in the service of their royal uncle, are they not written in the books of the chronicles of the civil wars of England?

After the execution of Charles the First Rupert received a new commission from Charles the Second, and continued to distinguish himself by sea and land; went to Portugal, the Mediterranean, the French coast, Madeira, the Azores, etc. etc.; encountered all kinds of dangers and vicissitudes, reverses and successes. A more chequered life is scarcely on record than that of Prince Rupert.

Our space is too limited to admit of any lengthened details of his adventures, 'moving accidents by flood and field,' and of all his 'hair-breadth 'scapes'; but one passage in his life is too full of romantic interest, and so characteristic of the fraternal affection of the Palatine Princes, to be passed over in silence. Captain Fearnes, who commanded the fine ship *The Admiral*, gives a noble and touching description of the incidents connected with the wreck of his vessel. One of the most disastrous tempests ever recorded in a seaman's log overtook the English fleet, then cruising among the Western Islands, and after every endeavour had been made to save the ship without a chance of success, Captain Fearnes, who survived the wreck, gives the following report: 'It was resolved that the ship must be our grave, and every man very well resolved to die, and the minister told us that as many as would receive the Sacrament he would administer it, and desired that we would give him notice, when we saw we were past all hope, to come to the place appointed, there to receive it, and die all together.'

Prince Rupert, believing his last moments were at hand, waved his brother Maurice to bring his vessel, *The Honest*

Seaman, under the Admiral's stern, to bid his beloved brother an eternal farewell, to give him his last directions and express his last wishes. Maurice, regardless of his own safety, commanded his men to lower a boat, either to save Rupert, or to put him on board and let them die together. His officers refused, as they said it would be to their own destruction, and be of no avail in saving Rupert. They made, indeed, a feint of lowering the boat, but paid little heed to the agony of their commander. Then the crew of *The Admiral* came to a noble decision. Deeply touched by the devotion which his Highness displayed, they conjured him to seek safety in the one little boat that was left them. This he steadily refused, saying 'that as they had run all risks with him, so he would participate them.' Thus did either try to breathe their last in unspeakable magnanimity. The brave seamen were not to be foiled; they elected a crew of undaunted lads, hoisted out their boat, and by force thrust their brave Prince into the same. He was put aboard *The Honest Seaman*, and immediately sent back the skiff to save as many as was possible, specifying the names of three officers, one of whom alone (and that the captain in command) accepted the offer. Fearnes was blamed by many for deserting his ship's company. He and the Prince's servant were boarded on one of the vessels, but the unfortunate little skiff was swamped. The Prince strove in vain to approach *The Admiral*, but it could not be done from stress of weather, and the doomed crew waved a sad farewell from the deck of the sinking ship to their comrades. In all, 333 men perished in this fatal storm, but the whole story remains a glorious passage in the annals of British seamen. Rupert's regret for the loss of a noble ship, with a rich freight on board, was little in comparison with his grief for that of his valued messmates. He was again threatened with a watery grave in a tremendous hurricane which overtook the fleet when at a short distance from the Virgin Islands, and in this fatal storm he had to deplore the loss of his devoted friend and brother, Prince Maurice, who went down on the deck of the well-named *Honest Seaman*. Yet once more he had an escape from drowning when at Paris at the Court of Louis the Fourteenth, in company with Charles the Second. A letter from a Roundhead thus details the circumstance :—

'The Seine had like to have made an end of your Black Prince Rupert' (he was swimming with the King and Duke of York); 'he was near being drowned if it had not been for the help of one of his servants, who dragged him up by the hair of his head.' These 'highly liveried blackamoors,' like all other dependants of the Prince, were much attached to their noble master.

On his return to England in 1662 Rupert seems to have given himself up to the pursuit of philosophical and scientific studies, even (so it was affirmed by many) to those of an occult nature. He fitted up for himself a workshop in the High Tower of Windsor Castle, furnished with forges, crucibles, retorts, instruments of all sorts, and here 'the hero of a hundred fights' might be seen with blacksmith's apron and bare brawny arms indulging in all the experiments of vital interest to a chemist and an alchemist. In this laboratory he was frequently visited by his royal cousin the King, and his favourite the Duke of Buckingham, both of whom took a great delight in Rupert's occupations. This strange man had other apartments assigned to him in the castle, where he kept stores of armour and weapons from all parts of the world, together with a library of valuable books, the catalogue of which is still extant. John Evelyn was a great admirer of Rupert's versatile talents, and was a delighted listener when the Prince related to him the discovery that he had made of mezzotint engraving. The story is well known how on one occasion, when at Brussels, the Prince observed a sentinel at some distance from his post very busy doing something to his piece. Rupert asked what he was about; he replied the dew had fallen in the night, had made his fusil rusty, and that he was scraping and cleaning it. The Prince, examining the gun, was struck with something like a figure eaten into the barrel with innumerable little holes closed together like friezed work on gold or silver, part of which the soldier had scraped away. This suggested to the Prince a contrivance which resulted in the discovery of mezzotint engraving, carried out in company with his protégé, the painter, Wallerant Vaillant. Great rivalry was excited on the occasion, and many people laid claim to an invention which was clearly that of Rupert.

Other discoveries and inventions of this wonderful man we leave to his more complete biographers. He found time in the midst of these engrossing pursuits to become enamoured of the charms of Francisca Bard, daughter of Lord Bellamont, by whom he had a son, on whose education he bestowed much care. He was called Dudley Bard, and grew up to emulate his father's military ardour and undaunted courage, but was killed at the siege of Buda in 1686, having just attained his twentieth year.

Negotiations were carried on at one time for an alliance between Rupert and a member of a royal house, but came to an end in consequence of the Prince's slender means.

In 1660 he once more embarked to oppose the French, alternating his beloved studies with his military and naval duties, but an old wound he had received in the head some time before put him to great torture and endangered his life, so much so that he was obliged to be trepanned. Requiring rest after the operation, he joined the Merry Monarch's merry Court at Tunbridge Wells, and had not long been there before he formed a connection with the fair Mistress Hughes, an actress belonging to the King's company, and one of the earliest female performers, who began her theatrical career in

1663, and gained great distinction in the character of Desdemona. The fascinations of this lady had a softening and refining influence on the manners and habits of his Highness, and even his beloved studies were neglected for the delights of her society. His dress was no longer neglected, and he vied with the other courtiers of his royal cousin in gallantry and compliments, but the beautiful comedian was not so easy of access as most of her compeers, and it was some time before she was induced to listen to her royal lover's suit. He was most lavish in his expenditure, grudging nothing to the fair siren. He purchased for her the magnificent seat of Sir Nicholas Crispe, near Hammersmith, afterwards the residence of the Margrave of Brandenburg, which cost £25,000 in the building.

By her he had a daughter named Ruperta, married to General Howe, of whom there is a most characteristic portrait in the collection of the Earl of Sandwich at Hinchingbrook. Mrs. Hughes remained on the stage for many years after Prince Rupert's death, who saw little of her in his later days, but bequeathed a large property to her and her daughter.

After leaving Tunbridge Wells he returned to Windsor, and resumed his studies, until called once more into active service. In 1673 he was appointed Lord High Admiral in place of the Duke of York, and commanded the fleet against the United Provinces, when, as usual, he distinguished himself. On the 29th of November 1682 Prince Rupert died in his house at Spring Gardens, 'mourned and respected' by men of the most differing interests. A magnificent funeral was allotted to him, and he was buried in Westminster Abbey.

Count Grammont, in his Memoirs, gives anything but a flattering description of the Prince's personal appearance, but we are more inclined to credit the testimony of such painters as Honthorst, Lely, and Kneller, whose portraits are undoubtedly noble and prepossessing.

No. 33.

LADY DIANA RUSSELL AS A CHILD.

Elizabethan ruff. Elaborate lace head-dress. Rich frock. Coral and bells. Holds a pack of cards.

DIED 1701.

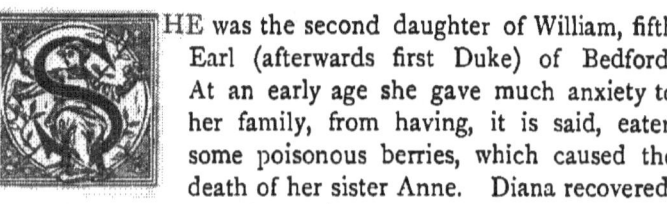HE was the second daughter of William, fifth Earl (afterwards first Duke) of Bedford. At an early age she gave much anxiety to her family, from having, it is said, eaten some poisonous berries, which caused the death of her sister Anne. Diana recovered, and married, in 1667, Sir Greville Verney of Compton Verney, County Warwick; and secondly, William, third Baron Allington of Wymondley and Killard, of Horseheath, County Cambridge, Constable of the Tower. Lady Allington appears to have taken a keen interest in the passing events of the day, especially in the Revolution of 1688. She is often mentioned in terms of genuine affection by Rachel, Lady Russell, in her letters.

DRAWING-ROOM.

DRAWING-ROOM.

No. 1. LADY ISABELLA DORMER, AFTERWARDS COUNTESS OF MOUNTRATH, AS A CHILD.

Tawny dress. Blue drapery. Fastening up a flower.

By Sir Peter Lely.

SHE was the second daughter of Charles, third Lord Dormer, and second and last Earl of Carnarvon (of that family), by Elizabeth, daughter of Arthur, Lord Capel. She married Sir Charles Coote, fourth Earl of Mountrath, of a noble family of French extraction, which settled first in Devonshire, and subsequently in Ireland. Sir Charles Coote, for his loyalty and military services, was, at the Restoration, created, with other honours, Earl of Mountrath. It was his grandson, and third Earl of Mountrath, who married the subject of this notice. He was much considered at Court, carried the banner of Ireland at the funeral of Queen Mary in 1694, was one of the Lords Justices in 1696, and died in 1709. His grandson, the sixth Earl, married Lady Diana Newport, daughter of the Earl of Bradford.

No. 2.   LADY DIANA FEILDING.

Oval. Blue dress. Dark hair.

DIED 1731.

BY SIR PETER LELY.

SHE was the daughter of Francis Newport, first Earl of Bradford, by Lady Diana Russell. She married, first, Thomas Howard of Ashtead, County Surrey, Esq., Knight of the Bath, Groom of the Bedchamber to George the First, Auditor of the Exchequer, and Clerk Comptroller of the Board of Green Cloth, by whom she had a son, who died while a schoolboy at Westminster, and a daughter married to Lord Dudley and Ward. By her second husband, the Honourable William Feilding, younger son of William, fifth Earl of Denbigh, and second Earl of Desmond (whom she also survived), she left no children. A marble tablet, surmounted by a bust, at Ashtead, where she lies buried, bears this inscription: 'Be this monument sacred to the memory of Lady Diana Feilding, daughter of Francis Newport, first Earl of Bradford. Her first husband was grandson to the Earl of Berkshire. Surviving her children, this illustrious branch of the house of Howard became her family. To it during her life she assured the inheritance of that estate she enjoyed by the bounty of her first husband, and at her death she made provision still more ample to support the honour and dignity of the present Earl of Berkshire and his descendants. That his gratitude therefore may be preserved in the minds of his latest posterity, Henry Bowes, Earl of Berkshire, has caused this monument to be erected, 1773.' Lady Diana was very charitable to the poor, and built and endowed alms-houses for six poor widows in the neighbourhood of Leatherhead.

Drawing-Room.

No. 3.   LADY DIANA RUSSELL.

Oval. Blue velvet gown. Pearl necklace. Fair curls.

BORN 1622, DIED 1694.

BY VERELST.

SHE was the youngest daughter of Francis William, son of William, Lord Russell of Thornhaugh, County North Hants, who succeeded his cousin Edward, as fourth Earl of Bedford. Her mother was Catherine, daughter and co-heir of Giles Bridges, Lord Chandos. Lady Diana married Francis, Viscount Newport (afterwards first Earl of Bradford), a distinguished loyalist, and brave soldier in Charles the First's army. He was taken prisoner at Oswestry in 1644, at which time his wife (with Lady D'Aubigny and others) also fell into the hands of the rebels, as appears by a letter from the famous Hugh Peters to the Earl of Stamford, soliciting the release of Lady Newport. She died in 1694, and was interred at Chenies, the burial-place of the Russell family in Buckinghamshire.

No. 4.   PORTRAIT OF A LADY.   UNKNOWN.

Dark blue dress. Seated, leaning her arm on a boulder. Landscape in the background.

BY SIR PETER LELY.

LIBRARY.

LIBRARY.

No. 1.

HONOURABLE ORLANDO BRIDGEMAN, GRENADIER GUARDS.

Undress. Guard's uniform.

BORN 1794, DIED 1827.

BY SIR GEORGE HAYTER.

HE was the third son of the first Earl of Bradford by the Hon. Lucy Byng. Was in the Grenadier Guards, and wounded at the battle of Waterloo, and at first reported dead. He married, in 1817, Lady Selina Needham, daughter of Francis, first Earl of Kilmorey, by whom he had three children.

No. 2.

CAPTAIN THE HONOURABLE CHARLES ORLANDO BRIDGEMAN, R.N.

Naval uniform. Holding a telescope.

BORN 1791, DIED 1860.

BY SIR GEORGE HAYTER.

He was the second son of Orlando, first Earl of Bradford (of the Bridgeman family), by Lucy Elizabeth Byng, daughter of George, fourth Viscount Torrington. He entered the Navy in 1804 as first-class volunteer, on board the *Repulse*, Captain the Honourable Arthur Legge, under whom the following year he became Midshipman, and was present at Sir Robert Calder's action at the Passage of the Dardanelles, and also in the Expedition of the Scheldt. In 1809 he joined the *Manilla*, 36, Captain George Francis Seymour (grandfather to the present Marquis of Hertford, 1885); in 1810 he was confirmed Lieutenant in the *Semiramis*, both on the Lisbon station. He was subsequently appointed Flag-Lieutenant to his old Commander, Rear-Admiral Legge, under whose orders he had first sailed. Charles Bridgeman was present at the defence of Cadiz, and joined successively the *Bellerophon*, hoisting the flag of Sir Richard Keats, on the Newfoundland station, and the *Royal Sovereign*, yacht, Captain Sir John Poer Beresford. For two years he then commanded the *Badger*, in the West Indies station, and assisted in the reduction of Guadaloupe, and later on was appointed to the *Icarus*, in South America, and the *Ruttenheimer*, which was attached to the squadron in the Mediterranean.

Charles Bridgeman retired from active service in 1846, attaining the rank of Vice-Admiral before his death. He married, in 1819, Elizabeth Anne, daughter of Sir Henry Chamberlain, British Consul at Rio Janeiro, by whom he had a family of three sons and five daughters. Charles Bridgeman was remarkable for his personal beauty, and was deservedly popular in the service.

No. 3.

THE HONOURABLE SELINA FORESTER, PRESENT COUNTESS OF BRADFORD.

Black gown. Small dog in her lap.

By Francis Grant, afterwards Sir Francis Grant, P.R.A.

HE youngest of the five beautiful daughters of the first Baron Forester, by Lady Katherine Manners, second daughter of the fourth Duke of Rutland. She married, in 1844, Viscount Newport, who succeeded his father as third and present Earl of Bradford, by whom she had four sons and two daughters.

No. 4.

PORTRAIT, SAID TO BE KING RICHARD THE THIRD.

PAINTER UNKNOWN.

No. 5. ROBERT JENKINSON, SECOND EARL OF LIVERPOOL, K.G.

Dark coat. White waistcoat.

BORN 1770, DIED 1828.

BY SIR GEORGE HAYTER.

BEGAN his education at a school at Parsonsgreen, where he remained till he was thirteen, and was then removed to the Charterhouse, where he continued for two or three years, and distinguished himself in classics and other branches of learning. He afterwards entered Christ Church College, Oxford, but his father had early destined him for public life, and directed Robert's studies with a view to his future career, making a point that political science, commerce, and finance should be especially attended to. At college young Jenkinson became the companion and friend of George Canning, afterwards Prime Minister, a friendship which continued for a very long period. Robert Jenkinson was at Paris on the breaking out of the Revolution, and witnessed the demolition of the Bastille by the mob: he was the means of affording useful information to the British Government respecting the state of

French public affairs, being in close correspondence with Mr. Pitt. On his return to England he was chosen Member of Parliament for Rye, under the especial patronage of the Minister. But his election taking place twelve months before his age qualified him to sit in the House of Commons, he passed the intervening time in Paris. In 1791, on attaining his twenty-first year, he took his seat, and made his first speech in opposition to a motion of Mr. Whitbread's on foreign affairs, in which the young member showed a wonderful acquaintance with European politics and international law. Both he and his father were opposed to the Abolition of the Slave-trade. When in 1792 Charles Fox moved an address to the King to the effect that his Majesty should send an Ambassador to the French Republic (Lord Gower having been recalled), Mr. Jenkinson, in the absence of Mr. Pitt, replied in indignant and eloquent terms : 'On this very day, while we are here debating about sending an Ambassador to Paris—on this very day is the King of France to receive sentence ; and in all probability it is the day of his murder.' And he proceeded in glowing terms to point out how ill-advised, undignified, and unfeeling the sanction which would thus be given to 'sanguinary monsters' would appear in the sight of all men. Fox's motion was rejected without a division, and Jenkinson's eloquence gained him universal praise, Edmund Burke being loud in his approbation. The young member rose in the opinion of all parties from that moment, and continued to take a prominent part as an upholder of the Government, which course he pursued for several years. In 1793 he was appointed one of the Commissioners of the India Board: he invariably distinguished himself, especially when speaking on matters connected with trade and commerce, for which, Mr. Sheridan said, ' Mr. Jenkinson might be expected to have some claims to hereditary knowledge.' In 1796 Robert's father was created Earl of Liverpool, and he himself assumed the title of Lord Hawkesbury. He was a staunch advocate for the union with Ireland, and in 1801 he became Foreign Secretary, on the formation of a new Ministry, which gave him ample scope for his knowledge of political affairs on the Continent ; and in the fulfilment of his official duties, he gained new laurels on many occasions too numerous to detail here. Later on, the management of the House of Commons (as it is technically called) devolved upon Lord Hawkesbury, who spoke on all the important questions of the day, and, at the opening of the next session, was called up to the House of Lords in order to strengthen the Ministry in the Upper House. On the return of Mr. Pitt at the head of the Ministry, he received the seals of the Home Department. At a late period of this session, on Mr. Wilberforce again bringing forward his favourite question of the Abolition of the Slave-trade, Lord Hawkesbury was instrumental in opposing the measure in the House of Lords, after it had passed the Commons, a course which he also pursued with regard to the Emancipation of the Roman Catholics of Ireland, advocated by Lord Grenville. On the death of Mr. Pitt in 1806, the King sent for Lord Hawkesbury to form a new Ministry, an offer which he deemed it advisable to decline, accepting, however, the office of Warden of the Cinque Ports. He afterwards resumed his old post as Home Secretary, and, his father dying in 1808, he succeeded to the Earldom of Liverpool. He warmly advocated the cause of Spain, and was selected to move the thanks of the House of Lords to Lord Wellington for his gallantry in the Peninsula. After the assassination of Mr. Perceval in 1812, Lord Liverpool was prevailed upon, after frequent refusals, to accept the office of Prime Minister, and during his long administration, which lasted from 1812 to 1827, many of the questions of the deepest importance connected with home and foreign politics were brought under the notice of the Government. Lord

Liverpool never slackened in his attention to public affairs, whatever difference of opinion may have existed then, or subsequently as to the liberality of his opinions. The last occasion on which Lord Liverpool was seen at his post was on the 15th of February 1827, when he moved an address expressing the willingness of the House to make an additional provision for the Duke and Duchess of Clarence. On the next day, after rising apparently in good health, and reading his morning letters, he was found by his servant stretched lifeless on the floor, and when the three most eminent physicians of the day were called in, it was ascertained that Lord Liverpool was suffering from an attack of an apoplectic and paralytic nature. As soon as prudence allowed, he was removed to his house at Combe Wood, where he gradually declined, both in mental and bodily power, and expired, in the presence of his wife, and his brother and successor, the Honourable Charles Cecil Jenkinson, on the 4th of December 1828.

Lord Liverpool was twice married: first, to Lady Louisa Hervey, third daughter of the Bishop of Derry, fourth Earl of Bristol, who died in 1821; and secondly, to Mary, daughter of Charles Chester, Esq., formerly Bagot, brother of the first Lord Bagot. He had no children by either marriage.

No. 6.

NAPOLEON BUONAPARTE THE FIRST: EMPEROR OF FRANCE.

Dark green uniform.

BY DAVID.

Biographical Catalogue.

No. 7.

GEORGE AUGUSTUS FREDERICK HENRY, SECOND EARL OF BRADFORD.

Blue coat. White waistcoat. Cloak.

BORN 1789, DIED 1865.

BY SIR GEORGE HAYTER.

HE was the eldest son of the first Earl of Bradford by the Hon. Lucy Byng. He married, first, Georgina, only daughter of Sir Thomas Moncreiffe, Bart., by whom he had several children; and secondly, Helen, widow of Sir David Moncreiffe, Bart., and daughter of Æneas Mackay, Esq., who died at Cannes in 1869.

No. 8.

ANNE BOLEYN, SECOND WIFE OF KING HENRY THE EIGHTH.

Large cap. Gown cut square.

EXECUTED 1536.

THIS is a crayon sketch by Holbein, with a memorandum in his own handwriting.

No. 9.

ORLANDO, FIRST EARL OF BRADFORD.

BORN 1762, DIED 1825.

By Sir George Hayter.

HE was the second Baron Bradford, and promoted to the Earldom in 1815. He married, in 1788, the Hon. Lucy Byng, daughter of George, fourth Viscount Torrington.

No. 10.

QUEEN VICTORIA.

A Sketch by Thomas.

Executed for Orlando, Lord Bradford, when Lord Chamberlain, by Her Majesty's Permission.

No. 11.

GEORGE THE SECOND, KING OF ENGLAND.

Red coat. Ribbon of the Garter.

BORN 1683, CROWNED KING OF ENGLAND 1727, DIED 1760.

By Pine.

No. 13.

EDWARD STANLEY, FOURTEENTH EARL OF DERBY, K.G.

*Black frock-coat. White waistcoat. Right hand on a table.
Left holds the string of eye-glass.*

BORN 1799, DIED 1869.

BY SIR FRANCIS GRANT, P.R.A.

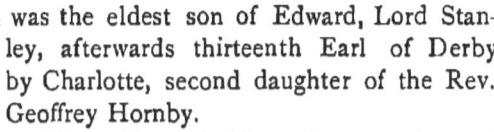

E was the eldest son of Edward, Lord Stanley, afterwards thirteenth Earl of Derby by Charlotte, second daughter of the Rev. Geoffrey Hornby.

The subject of this notice was educated at Eton and Christ Church, Oxford, where in 1819 he gained the Chancellor's prize for Latin verse for his poem of *Syracuse.* In 1821 he entered the House of Commons as member for Stockbridge, and sat subsequently for Preston, Windsor, and North Lancashire. He was Under-Secretary for the Colonies from 1830 to 1833, Secretary of State for the Colonies from 1833 to 1834, and again from 1841 to 1845. In 1844 he was summoned to the House of Lords in his father's barony of Stanley, and in 1859 was made a K.G. He was First Lord of the Treasury in 1852, 1858, and 1866. He was a strenuous opposer of Free-trade and the Repeal of the Corn Laws, and his name is invariably connected with 'Protection.' Lord Derby was remarkable as a statesman, a scholar, a wit, and an orator. In the latter capacity his enthusiasm and eloquence gained him the sobriquet of 'the Rupert of Debate.' In society his brilliant conversation, keen sense of humour, and genial disposition, made him a favourite with men and women of all classes and opinions, and his death was as much deplored in private as in political circles.

Library.

He married, in 1825, Emma Caroline, second daughter of Edward, first Lord Skelmersdale, who survived him, and by whom he had two sons and a daughter.

This little picture is the original design of Sir F. Grant for a large portrait of Lord Derby, which was painted for the family, and he afterwards finished it with great care, and gave it to Lord Bradford.

No. 15.

HENRY GRESWOLD LEWIS, ESQ. OF MALVERN HALL.

DIED 1819.

BY CONSTABLE.

HE married the Honourable Charlotte Bridgeman, daughter of Henry, Lord Bradford.

No. 16.

THE HONOURABLE AND REVEREND GEORGE BRIDGEMAN.

Black coat.

BORN 1765, DIED 1832.

BY CONSTABLE.

E was the youngest son of Henry, first Lord Bradford, by the daughter and heir of the Rev. John Simpson. He entered the Church, and held successively the family livings of Weston, and Wigan (in Lancashire), where he died.

In 1792 he married Lady Lucy Boyle, only daughter

of Edmund, seventh Earl of Cork and Orrery, by whom he had two daughters and one son. Lady Lucy died in 1801, and in 1809 the widower married Charlotte Louisa, daughter of William Poyntz, Esq. of Midgham, Berks, who was first cousin to his first wife. This lady had no children, and she died in 1840, at Hampton Court. Mr. Bridgeman was a most amiable man and a most genial companion. He was beloved in his own family, and among a large circle of friends, by the servants of his household, the poor in his parish, by children, horses, and dogs. Indeed, the influence he exercised over animals was wonderful. In his latter days he possessed a beautiful thoroughbred chestnut mare, hot-tempered and violent by nature, who let no opportunity slip of taking the bit between her teeth. The grooms, until they became 'up to her wicked ways,' fought shy of riding her, and the writer's sister, a splendid and fearless horsewoman, was very much mortified one day at finding she could not hold 'uncle George's' mare. Yet the moment Mr. Bridgeman, then old and infirm, got into the saddle, the generous beast became as quiet as a lamb, and her master would often lay the reins on her beautiful neck, to show the perfect understanding that subsisted between them. Added to an earnest and by no means morose piety, the good pastor possessed a vein of genial humour, and a genuine love of fun, which was doubtless one of the qualities that endeared him to the younger part of the community, and an anecdote is told of him which is highly characteristic. One evening, dining alone at a club in London, where he was little known, it was impossible to avoid overhearing the conversation at a neighbouring table, which, strangely enough, turned on his own son, an officer of the Guards. The diners spoke of the pecuniary difficulties into which he had lately been plunged, and while they confessed his extravagance, they sang his praises—at least he was not selfish, at least he spent his money on others, etc. etc.; no doubt about it, Bridgeman was a capital fellow, the best fellow in the world, and many were the jolly parties they had had at his expense. Now this was a sore subject at that moment to the Rector of Wigan, but his sense of the ludicrous triumphed over every other feeling, and, rising quietly, he advanced towards the astonished group at the other table. 'Gentlemen,' he said, 'I am very grateful for the handsome terms in which you have spoken of my son, but will you allow me to remark that it is I who am the best fellow in the world, since it is I who have paid for all those dinners and suppers, which I am delighted to think you have so much enjoyed.'

No. 17.

THE HONOURABLE JOHN BRIDGEMAN SIMPSON.

Brown coat. White waistcoat.

BORN 1763, DIED 1850.

AFTER HOPPNER. *The Original is at Babworth.*

E was the second son of Henry Bridgeman, first Baron Bradford, of Weston under Lizard, by the daughter and heir of the Rev. John Simpson of Babworth, County Notts. In 1784 he married Henrietta Frances, daughter and heir of Sir Thomas Worsley, Bart., by whom (who died in 1791) he had, besides two children who died young, a daughter who became heir to her uncle, Sir Richard Worsley, and married the Honourable Charles Pelham, afterwards Lord Yarborough. John Bridgeman assumed the maternal arms and name of Simpson in 1785, and eventually inherited the property of that family. In 1793 he married, as his second wife, Grace, daughter of Samuel Estwicke, Esq., by whom he had a very numerous family.

No. 18. SIR GEORGE GUNNING, BART.
Dark coat.
BORN 1783, DIED 1823.
BY CONSTABLE.

E was the eldest son of Sir Robert Gunning, Bart., K.B., of Horton, County North Hants, by Anne, only daughter of Robert Sutton, Esq. of Scofton, County Notts. Sir Robert had resided some time at the Courts of Berlin and St. Petersburg, as Minister Plenipotentiary, and was created a Baronet for his diplomatic services. His son and successor, George, married the daughter of Henry Bridgeman, first Lord Bradford, in 1794. Sir George represented the boroughs of Wigan, Hastings, and East Grinstead, at different periods in Parliament.

No. 19. SIR WILLIAM LOWTHER, BART.
Brown coat. White waistcoat. Right hand holding a fold of the coat. White frill.
DIED 1763 (?).
BY SIR JOSHUA REYNOLDS.

E was the son of Sir Thomas Lowther of Holker Hall, by Lady Elizabeth Cavendish (called in the family Lady Betty), daughter of the second Duke of Devonshire.

A note in Sir Joshua Reynolds' handwriting says that he made three copies of the portrait of Sir William Lowther: one for Major Kynaston, one for Mr. Bridgeman, and one for Lord Frederick Cavendish, Lady Elizabeth's nephew, in 1758. He died unmarried, and left all the Holker property to Lord George Cavendish, on whose death in 1794 the estates devolved on the Duke of Devonshire, and are now in possession of the present Duke (1888). Sir William Lowther was a man of refined taste, had travelled much in Italy, and made an excellent collection of pictures, respecting the purchase of which he gives some amusing details in letters which are still extant at Holker.

No. 20. VICE-ADMIRAL LORD HUGH SEYMOUR.
Naval uniform.
BORN 1759, DIED 1801.
BY HOPPNER.

E was the fifth son of Francis, Earl, afterwards Marquis, of Hertford, by a daughter of the Duke of Grafton. He entered the Roya Navy while yet a boy, and justified his parents' choice of a profession for him, never losing an opportunity of distinguishing himself in the service he loved. His first cruise was on board the *Pallas*, Captain the Honourable Leveson Gower.

In 1785 he married Lady Horatia Waldegrave, daughter of James, second Earl Waldegrave, with whose beautiful features we are well acquainted in Sir Joshua Reynolds' world-famed picture of 'The Three Sisters,' so long the glory of Strawberry Hill. The union was very happy, only marred by the separations which Lord Hugh's profession entailed; they had a family of five sons and three daughters. Seymour gained post-rank early, and in 1794 did good service in command of the *Leviathan*, on the glorious 1st of June (Lord Howe's victory), when he was promoted to a colonelcy of marines. Next year he attained flag-rank, and commanded the *Spaniel*, under Lord Bridport, in that Admiral's encounter with the French fleet off the island of St. Croix. From 1795 to 1798 Lord Hugh had a seat at the Board of Admiralty, after which he was appointed Commander-in-Chief of the Leeward Islands, during which time the colony of Surinam surrendered to the English combined naval and military forces under Admiral Lord Hugh Seymour and General Trigge. The Admiral's eldest son, afterwards Admiral Sir George Seymour, whose son succeeded to the Marquisate of Hertford, was on board his father's ship, but was invalided home in 1801, and on his arrival in England sad news awaited him. His beloved mother was no more; while a fast sailing ship brought the fatal tidings that a few days after his own departure, Lord Hugh had died of yellow fever. Yet another blow was in store for the poor young sailor, enfeebled by illness, and nearly overwhelmed by this accumulation of sorrow, in the loss of his favourite little brother, William, the pet of the family. The tenderest care and most consummate skill were needed to snatch George Seymour from the jaws of death. But he lived to be an honour to his profession, and a blessing to his family and friends. He inherited his mother's beauty, as those who remember him can testify. His countenance was noble, his eyes large and brilliant, while even the wide gash of a sabre cut, received in action, across the lips, was powerless to mar the rare sweetness of his smile.

No. 21. HENRY, FIRST LORD BRADFORD.

Peer's Parliamentary robes. White hair.

DIED 1800.

BY ROMNEY (?).

[See page 188.]

No. 22. GEORGE BRIDGEMAN, ESQ.

Uniform Grenadier Guards. Scarlet cloak.

BORN 1727, DIED 1767.

BY SIR JOSHUA REYNOLDS.

HE was the third son of Sir Orlando Bridgeman, by Lady Ann Newport, daughter and heiress of the second Earl of Bradford. He died unmarried at Lisbon.

No. 23.

CAPTAIN JOHN WILLETT PAYNE, R.N., AFTERWARDS VICE-ADMIRAL.

Naval uniform.

BORN 1752, DIED 1803.

BY HOPPNER.

E entered the Royal Navy in 1769, on board the *Quebec*, thirty-two guns, Captain Lord Ducie; then served in the *Eagle*, sixty-four guns, bearing the flag of Earl Howe, during the American war, whence he was made Lieutenant, and afterwards promoted to post-rank, July 1780.

Captain Payne distinguished himself on several occasions, especially in an engagement in the West Indies, in 1783, with the *Pluto*, a ship of very superior force. He was in command of the *Russell*, in Lord Howe's memorable victory, the glorious 1st of June 1794. In 1799 he became Rear-Admiral of the *Red*, and the following year succeeded Lord Bridport as Treasurer of Greenwich Hospital. He brought over Caroline of Brunswick, Princess of Wales, on board the *Jupiter*. Jack Payne, as he was called in society, was a great favourite and constant companion of the Prince of Wales, who appointed him Comptroller of his Household, in which capacity he made himself extremely popular by his courtesy, geniality, and genuine kindness. At the time of his death he had also the command (being then Vice-Admiral) of the coasts of Devonshire and Cornwall, and Lord Warden of the Stannaries.

He died at Greenwich, whence he was followed to the grave by an interminable procession of carriages, many of which contained friends and acquaintances, for Admiral Payne was a most popular member of society. He was buried in St. Margaret's, Westminster.

No. 24.

THE HONOURABLE ORLANDO GEORGE CHARLES BRIDGEMAN, THIRD EARL OF BRADFORD.

When a child. In a red frock. Sitting on the lawn.

BORN 1819.

BY SIR GEORGE HAYTER, R.A.

E is the eldest son of the second Earl of Bradford (of the Bridgeman family), by Georgina, the only daughter of Sir Thomas Moncreiffe, Bart. Educated at Harrow School and at Trinity College, Cambridge; was M.P for Shropshire, from 1842 until he succeeded to the Earldom in 1865; was Vice-Chamberlain of the Royal Household from February till December 1852, and from February 1858 till June 1859; Lord Chamberlain from 1866 till December 1868; and Master of the Horse to the Queen from 1874 till May 1880; and again from June 1885 till Feb. 1886. He is Deputy-Lieutenant of Staffordshire, and Deputy-Lieutenant of Warwickshire; Captain of the Salopian Yeomanry, 1844, and Lieutenant-Colonel of 1st Battalion of

Shropshire Volunteers; also Lord-Lieutenant and *Custos Rotulorum* of Shropshire since 1875.

In 1844 he married the Honourable Selina Forester, youngest daughter of the first Lord Forester, by Lady Katherine Manners, second daughter of the fourth Duke of Rutland.

DINING-ROOM.

DINING-ROOM.

No. 1. MARGARET HOWARD, COUNTESS OF CARLISLE, AND HER NIECE, LADY DIANA RUSSELL.

Reddish brown gown. Resting her hand on a table. Little girl in a white frock leaning against her aunt's knee.

BORN 1618.   DIED 1664.

BY STONE AFTER VANDYCK.

HE was the third daughter of Francis, fourth Earl of Bedford, by Catherine Brydges. She married at a very early age James Hay, afterwards second Earl of Carlisle, of that family. Margaret's father-in-law was often connected with her own father in the political events of the reign of Charles the First. After the death of her husband in 1660, she married her second lord, Robert Rich, Earl of Warwick, second Earl of Holland; and lastly, Edward Montagu, Earl of Manchester, of whom Clarendon speaks in terms of high eulogium. The little girl in the picture is Lady Diana Russell, afterwards Lady Allington.

No. 3. THOMAS, EARL OF ARUNDEL AND SURREY.

In armour. With a boy beside him.

BORN 1592. DIED 1646.

By VANDYCK.

ESPECTING this picture there has been more than one controversy, and it has been not only erroneously named in a catalogue of a gallery at Madrid, but copied, doubtless from thence, into the edition of engravings of Vandyck's portraits in the British Museum. It has been miscalled Don Alonzo Perez de Guzman el Bueno and his son. The late Lord Bradford, when in Madrid, saw a replica of the picture in his possession, and made a note to the effect that the portrait could not be that of the Spanish nobleman in question, according to the date of Vandyck's death. His lordship identified it as that of Thomas, Earl of Arundel and Surrey, and his grandson.

Thomas was the only son of Philip, Earl of Arundel (who died a prisoner in the Tower), by Anne, sister and co-heir of Thomas, Lord Dacre of Gillesland. He was deprived, by his father's attainder, of the honours and greater part of the estates of his family, and had only the title of Lord Maltravers by courtesy during Queen Elizabeth's reign, but was restored by Act of Parliament in the first year of James the First (1603) to all the titles and estates which his father had enjoyed before his attainder, as also to the Earldom of Surrey, and to such dignity of baronies as his grandfather, the Duke of Norfolk, had also forfeited. He was, moreover, created Earl Marshal in 1621, and Earl of Norfolk in 1644; he married Lady Alatheia Talbot, daughter, and eventually sole heir, of Gilbert, seventh Earl of Shrewsbury, and was succeeded by his second son, Henry Frederick.

No. 5. DOROTHY, COUNTESS OF SUNDERLAND.

Crimson dress. Pearl ornaments. Pillar in the back-ground.

BORN 1620, DIED 1683-4.

BY VANDYCK.

IT has been well said of this beautiful and exemplary woman, that she is even (like the old Italian masters of painting) better known to posterity by her sobriquet than her name, for there were more than one Lady Sunderland, but only one 'Saccharissa.' The poet, therefore, may lay better claim to the title of godfather than the sponsors who held the infant Dorothy at the font. She was the eldest of the eight daughters of Robert Sidney, Earl of Leicester, of that name, by Dorothy, daughter of Henry Percy, ninth Earl of Northumberland. Lord and Lady Leicester bore a high character for 'integrity and refinement of breeding at the Court of Charles the First, while in private life they shone a bright example of domestic harmony.' Lady Leicester was a provident as well as a tender mother, and she entertained early projects in the matter of an advantageous marriage for her daughter, while Dorothy was still very young. At sixteen the girl was renowned for her beauty, and already surrounded by suitors. There appears to have been a talk at Court of the probability of a match with my Lord Russell, the heir of the house of Bedford; and Lady Leicester writes from the country to her lord at Court, in 1635: 'It would

rejoice me much to receave some hope of that lord's addresses to Doll, that you writt of to me, for next to what consarns you, I confess she is considered by me above any thing of this world.'

This marriage, however, was not to be, and there was shortly after a talk of the Earl of Devonshire, which, by Lady Leicester's correspondence, appears to have had some let or hindrance, through the interference of meddling interferers; beside, she considered his mother and sister were 'full of decaite and jugling,' professing to desire the union. The next aspirant to the fair hand of the beautiful daughter of Penshurst was no other than the celebrated Lord Lovelace, of whom her mother thus writes: 'I find my Lord Lovelace so uncertaine and so idle, so much addicted to mean companie, and easily drawn to debaucherie, it is now my studie to brake off with him. Many particulars I could tell you of his wildnesse, but the knowledge of them would be of no use to you, as he is likely to be a stranger to us. For tho' his estate is goode, his person pretie enowfe, his witte much more than ordinarie, yet dare I not venture to give Doll to him.' Lady Leicester concludes her letter to her husband by saying, 'My deere hart, let not these cross accidents trouble you, for we do not know what God has provided for her.'

The poet Waller now came forward and laid himself at the feet of the high-born beauty; he had been left a widower when quite young, and had gifts of nature and fortune to recommend him, but Dorothy's parents looked for noble birth in a suitor for their daughter's hand, and it is to be feared the poor poet was dismissed with some disdain. He was not inconsolable, however; he sought solace from his Muse, and, better still, in his union shortly afterwards with a willing bride.

A marriage was at length concluded 'for dear Doll,' which was calculated to satisfy the best expectations of her parents, and to ensure her own happiness.

Henry, Lord Spencer of Wormleighton, the first-born son of the second lord, by Penelope, daughter of Thomas Wriothesley, Earl of Southampton, was born at Althorp, his father's country house, in 1620. To that father's titles and large estates the young man succeeded in 1636, and in 1639 he was married at Penshurst, Lord Leicester's beautiful home in Kent, to that nobleman's eldest and most beloved daughter, Lady Dorothy Sidney. Lord Leicester was at the time Ambassador to the Court of France, and immediately after the marriage the happy young couple hurried off to join the bride's father in Paris, where they remained for two years, that is to say, until Lord Leicester's diplomatic mission was at an end. On their return, Lord Spencer took his seat in the House of Lords, and soon made himself an object of esteem and commendation by his talents and general good conduct. These qualities, added to his high position and large property, naturally made him an object worth contending for by the two adverse parties that were now beginning to convulse England. Lord Spencer had liberal views in the literal acceptation of the word, and stoutly opposed many measures which he considered arbitrary that emanated from the Throne; and the Parliament, which was now beginning to assume the executive, had great hopes of the young lord, and believed that they had bound him to their side when he accepted the Lord-Lieutenancy of his native county which they offered him. But Lord Spencer came of a loyal stock, and there is little doubt he cherished the hope of mediating between the King and his Parliament, in which expectation he had many sharers amongst the nobility and gentry of the land. He strove all he could to be a 'daysman' between the two factions, but finding that his admonitions to the Parliament when they broke out into open rebellion were of no avail, he proclaimed himself stoutly for the King; and in the early and blissful days of his married life he tore himself from the embrace of his beautiful wife and the calm happiness of his ancestral home, to mix in the noise, turmoil, and danger of a camp, in company with his kinsman and countyman, the gallant Spencer Compton, Earl of Northampton, who was destined to fall at Hopton Heath. Lord Spencer joined the King at York, and when the royal standard was unfurled at Nottingham, he took the field as a volunteer. In his constant letters to his 'dearest harte,' he gives a melancholy picture of the perplexed and unsatisfactory state of affairs in the royal army. He says: 'The discontent that I and other honest men receive dayly is beyond expression,' and he declares 'that were it not for the punctilio of honour' he would not 'remaine an howre.'

Lord Spencer was with the King at Edgehill, and with Prince Rupert at Bristol, etc. etc., and in 1643 he was raised to the dignity of Earl of Sunderland. He writes a long and most loving letter to his sweetest Doll from before Gloucester, and thanks her for her letters, 'writing to you and hearing from you being the most pleasant entertainment I am capable of receiving in anie place, but especially here, where, but when I am in the trenches (which are seldom without my company), I am more solitarie than ever I was in mie life.' In another letter written from Oxford in September 1643, he thus speaks of his little daughter: 'Pray bless Popet for me, and tell her I would have writt to her, but on deliberation I deem it uncivil to return an answer to a ladie in anie other characters but her own, and that I am not learned enough to do.' Alas! the brave soldier was never more destined to enjoy his wife's dear company, or clasp his sweet Popet to his heart. Four days after that letter was penned, the writer was struck down by a cannon ball on the field of Newbury, in company with his friend and brother in arms, 'the incomparable Falkland,' and many other brave and loyal spirits. For twelve months Lord Sunderland had fought beside the King, as a volunteer, for he never would accept a commission. There is a most touching letter extant from Lord Leicester to his widowed daughter, which our limited space alone prevents our inserting here. The fair hopes contained in her old admirer Waller's letter, written at the time of her marriage, to her sister, Lady Lucy Sidney, were far from being fulfilled. After wishing the couple every happiness, he says, ' May her lord not mourn her long, but go hand in hand with her to that place where is neither marrying nor giving in marriage, but being divorced, we may all have an equal interest in her.' There spoke the disappointed and jealous lover. Lady Sunderland was with child of a daughter at the period of her lord's untimely death, who scarcely survived its birth. She retired to her husband's estate in Northamptonshire, where she made herself generally beloved. ' She is not to be mentioned,' says Lloyd in his Memoirs of the Loyalists, ' without the highest honour, in the catalogue of sufferers, to so many of whom her house was a sanctuary, her interest a protection, her estate a maintenance.' Influenced, it is said, by her father's wishes, she contracted a second marriage in 1652 to Sir Robert Smythe, of the family of the Lords Strangford, a gentleman of Kent, but was again left a widow; she survived Sir Robert some time, and, we are told, she continued to see her old flame Waller, to whom she one day put the dangerous question—' Pray, Master Waller, when will you write such pretty verses to me again?' Was it the sting of old mortification which prompted the cruel answer, ' When your ladyship is young and beautiful again '? By her first husband Lady Sunderland had two children, Robert, the second Earl,— the Minister of whom the anecdote is told that when Addison intrusted Edmund Smith with the task of writing a history of the Revolution of 1688, the proposed author asked the staggering question, ' What shall I do with the character of Lord Sunderland?' and a daughter, Dorothy, who married Sir George Saville, afterwards Marquis of Halifax. By her second husband she had an only child, Robert, Governor of Dover Castle. Lady

Sunderland lies buried by the side of her dearly loved Henry in a beautiful monument, in the Spencer chapel, in the church of Brington, hard by Althorp House, and in that house her name is still a household word; and Saccharissa's bed, the curtains of which, having her embroidered monogram of S twisting round columns, may still be seen in one of the principal guest-chambers.

No. 7.

CHARLES THE FIRST, KING OF ENGLAND.

Front face and two profiles.

BORN 1600, SUCCEEDED 1625, EXECUTED 1649.

BY CARLO MARATTI AFTER VANDYCK.

HE second son of James the First, by Anne of Denmark. Married Henrietta Maria of France. Dethroned and beheaded by his subjects. The original of this picture by Vandyck, now at Windsor Castle, was sent to Rome to Bernini, in order that he might make a bust from the same; Carlo Maratti copied the picture while in the sculptor's studio. On first beholding the beautiful and noble head, the sculptor is said to have exclaimed, 'That is the portrait of one who is born to misfortune.'

No. 12.   VENETIAN COURTESAN.

BY TITIAN.

No. 14.

EDWARD SEYMOUR, FIRST DUKE OF SOMERSET, THE PROTECTOR.

Tight-fitting vest. Black hat.

EXECUTED 1552.

BY HOLBEIN.

HE second but eldest surviving son of Sir John Seymour, of Wulfhall, County Wilts, by Margaret, daughter of Sir John Wentworth of Nettlested, County Suffolk. He was educated at Oxford and Cambridge, and joining his father, who was in high favour at Court, entered the army, distinguished himself in France, and was knighted for his services in 1525. On his return to England he was appointed Esquire to the King, and was one of the challengers in the tilt-yard at Greenwich, when Henry the Eighth kept his Christmas there.

On the King's marriage with his sister, Jane Seymour, Edward was created Viscount Beauchamp, and in 1537 Earl of Hertford. He was then sent to France on a mission, and was created Knight Companion of the Garter, at Hampton Court, on his return. From this time his life became most eventful. He proceeded twice to Scotland, high in command, and again to France, where he was instrumental in concluding a peace with that country. Honours and distinctions too many to enumerate were heaped on the King's brother-in-law, even after the death of poor Queen Jane. He was one of the many executors of Henry the Eighth, by whose will he was appointed guardian to the young King, and so prompt were his measures and so successful his ambitious and self-seeking policy that when the nephew was proclaimed King in London, the uncle was appointed Protector of the realm. He already bore the titles of Earl and Viscount, and Edward the Sixth, not content with adding the title of Baron, bestowed a ducal coronet upon him, in order that the name of that family, 'from which our most beloved mother Jane, late Queen of England, drew her beginning, might not be clouded by any higher title or colour of dignity.' Thus ran the words of the patent. When the Duke of Norfolk was attainted, the Protector was made Earl Marshal for life. His power now became almost absolute, and the boy King, delighted to do his uncle honour, elected that he should sit on the right hand of the throne. Indeed Somerset was now king in all but name, and his enemies, of whom there were many, accused him of aspiring to the Crown in good earnest. It was alleged against him that he used the royal pronoun 'we,' and signed himself 'Protector by the grace of God.' But the life of Protector Somerset belongs to the chronicles of the history of England. Numerous factions rose up against him, at the head of which were the Earl of Warwick, his sworn enemy, and his own ungrateful brother, Thomas, Lord Seymour of Sudley. Many charges were brought against him; he was deprived of all his high offices, and imprisoned in the Tower. The young King, who loved him dearly, had little power to befriend his uncle, whose estates were forfeited, and he was treated with insult and contumely. The Earl of Warwick was bent on his destruction. Arraigned of high treason at Westminster Hall, he demanded a trial of his peers, was acquitted of the principal charge, but found guilty of felony, and after several months' imprisonment, in spite of every attempt on King Edward's part, Edward Seymour, Duke of Somerset, was condemned to die on the scaffold. On reaching the platform, he kneeled in prayer, and afterwards addressed the people, with the majority of whom he was a great favourite, in calm and measured terms, declaring his innocence, his loyalty to the King, and his love of his native country. A tumult took place among the people, and a horseman appearing suddenly in the crowd, a cry was raised of 'A pardon! a pardon!' But all the time his arch-enemy, Lord Warwick (or rather Northumberland, as he then was), stood by untouched, shaking his cap and making signs to the people to be quiet. We have not space to make extracts from a dying speech, which for manliness, forbearance, and piety could scarcely be surpassed. The Duke, unbuckling his sword, presented it to the Lieutenant of the Tower, gave the executioner money, bade all near him farewell, and then kneeling down, arranged his collar and covered his face, which showed 'no signs of trouble,' with his handkerchief. Laying his head upon the block, he called out thrice 'Lord Jesu, save me,' and then received the deathstroke.

Edward, first Duke of Somerset, was twice married. First, to Catherine, daughter and co-heir of Sir William Fillol, of Woodlands, County Dorset, respecting whom there exists a mystery and rumours of misconduct. Certain it is that her son was disinherited. There seems little doubt, at all events, that the Duke's second wife, the daughter of Sir Edward Stanhope, of Bampton, County Dorset, an ambitious and violent woman, worked on her husband's mind, to the detriment of her predecessor's children, in spite of which the coveted titles devolved after some generations on Catherine Fillol's descendants, ancestors in direct line to the present Duke of Somerset.

No. 16. PORTRAIT OF A LADY. UNKNOWN.

BY LUCAS CRANACH.

No. 18.

PORTRAIT OF A LADY WITH A MONKEY.

BY PARIS BORDONE (?).

No. 22. PORTRAIT OF A CHILD.

BY PAUL VERONESE.

No. 23. ANTHONY VANDYCK

As Paris.

BORN 1599, DIED 1641.

AFTER VANDYCK.

THE eldest son of a merchant in Antwerp (himself a painter in glass), by one Maria Cuypero. Little Anthony's mother was a skilful artist in embroidery, and encouraged her boy's taste for drawing, in the rudiments of which he received instruction from his father. When only ten years of age he became the pupil of Hendrik van Balen, a much-esteemed painter, who had studied in Italy; but young Vandyck had set his heart on entering the studio of his famous fellow-citizen, Peter Paul Rubens, and that desire was fulfilled. His remarkable talent and untiring industry made him a favourite both of master and scholars, when an incident happened which brought him into prominent notice. It chanced one afternoon, when Rubens was absent, that the scholars invaded the sanctity of the private studio, and, in the exuberance of animal spirits, indulged in what in modern parlance is called 'bear-fighting.' An unfinished Holy Family stood on an easel, the colours not yet dry, and, in the course of the rough play, one of his companions pushed Van Diepenbeke so heavily against the precious canvas that the arm of the Magdalen and the head of the Virgin were nearly effaced, and all the colours smudged. The general consternation may easily be conceived. A council was held, and a general decision arrived at that the most skilful among the students should endeavour to repair the mischief. Unanimous choice fell on Vandyck, who began to work in right earnest, for there was not a moment to lose. There were but a few hours of daylight left him, but he accomplished his task before nightfall. Early next morning the dreaded moment arrived. Rubens entered his studio in order to examine the work of the preceding evening, when he pronounced the memorable words which seemed to bestow a diploma on his young disciple: 'Why, this looks better than it did yesterday!' Then, approaching nearer, he detected the traces of a strange hand. Investigation and explanation followed, and Vandyck came in for great praise from the lips of his beloved master. Rubens was most desirous that his talented pupil should proceed to Italy to study the works of the great masters, but in the meantime the young man had received an invitation to England. The first visit he paid to our country was short and unsatisfactory, and there are so many discrepancies in the accounts of the work he did at that period and his reasons for leaving England somewhat abruptly, that we refrain from entering further on the subject. From England Vandyck proceeded to the Hague, where he painted portraits of every class and denomination of person, commencing with the Court and family of the Stadtholder, Henry Frederick. Nobles, warriors, statesmen, burghers, all vied for the honour of sitting to him. The news of his father's illness recalled him to Antwerp. He arrived just in time to receive that father's blessing, and listen to his last injunctions, which included an order to paint an altar for the Chapel of the Dominican Sisters, who had nursed him tenderly in his illness. After many delays from various causes Vandyck arrived in Venice, where he studied Titian and Veronese, and afterwards proceeded to Genoa, where he became the favourite of the proudest nobles of that proud city, and adorned almost every palace therein with splendid portraits. At Rome he remained some years; the first order he received being that of the world-renowned portrait of Cardinal Bentivoglio, which attracted a crowd of sitters to his studio, including all the nobility of the city and most of the foreign visitors. He then made his way to Florence and most of the northern cities of Italy, with a flying visit to Sicily, whence he was driven by the outbreak of the plague. He returned to Antwerp, where he at first shared the proverbial fate of the prophet in his own country, and met with much ill-will and small patronage, until his old friend Rubens came to his rescue by buying every completed picture in his late scholar's studio, and recommending and befriending him on every occasion. Shortly afterwards Rubens departed from Antwerp on a diplomatic mission, and he left Vandyck undisputed master of the field. His hands were now full; he received endless commissions both in portraits and sacred subjects. He afterwards went to Paris, and paid two visits to England; the second time he was received at Court with every mark of distinction. Charles the First treated the noble Fleming as a personal friend, taking the greatest delight in his society. He became the centre of attraction, and the cynosure of all eyes. Pre-eminently handsome, brilliant in conversation, a good linguist, an enlightened traveller—even without the crowning quality of his splendid talent, the painter became a shining light in the refined and aristocratic circles of the English capital. The King bestowed the honour of knighthood on him, and presented him with a valuable miniature of himself set in diamonds. Both their Majesties sat constantly for their portraits, and it is needless to observe that every country house in England is enriched by treasures from the brush of Vandyck. The King and the Duke of Buckingham were busy in arranging a suitable match for their friend and favourite. The lady selected was Mary Ruthven, a member of the Queen's household, and grand-daughter of the unfortunate Earl Gowrie, much esteemed for her goodness and beauty, who visited Antwerp with her husband shortly after their marriage, where they were received with every mark of respect and distinction. After this they went to Paris, where Vandyck met with disappointment, and fell into bad health, and on his return to England he found that country in a state of confusion and political strife, his royal and private friends involved in trouble and perplexity, the King and Queen both absent from London, and the Parliament in arms against the Crown. Sir Anthony's health declined, both physically and morally. He gave himself up to the pursuit of alchemy, and would stand for hours over a hot fire in the vain hope of obtaining the philosopher's stone; He grew haggard and wrinkled while still in the prime of life. The King, returning to London, and hearing of his friend's illness, sent his own physician, but all human aid was unavailing. A severe attack of gout, combined with other maladies, proved fatal, and on the 9th of December 1641, the man who by many has been considered the chief of the world's portrait painters breathed his last. Followed by a large retinue of friends, he was buried in St. Paul's Cathedral, leaving a most exemplary will, in which wife, child, sister, servants, were all remembered, as also the poor in two parishes. He left an only daughter, Justiniana, who married Sir John Stepney of Prendergast, Pembroke, and afterwards Martin de Carbonnell. She received a pension from King Charles the Second.

Lady Vandyck married a Welsh baronet, Sir Robert Pryce, as his second wife.

No. 25.   PORTRAIT OF A CHILD.

By Paul Veronese.

No. 26.   SIR NICHOLAS CAREW.

Black and white dress.

BEHEADED 1539.

By Holbein.

THE Carews came of an ancient family in Devonshire, but the branch to which Sir Nicholas belonged had settled at Beddington, in Surrey, an estate that had come into their possession by marriage.

Nicholas was the eldest son of Sir Richard Carew, Knight-Banneret, by Magdalen, daughter of Sir Thomas Oxenbridge, Bart., of Ford, in Sussex. When Sir Richard died, and his son succeeded, the landed property was very extensive, and it was said the owner might start from his own house, and ride in any direction straight on end for ten miles at least on his own land. When still a youth Nicholas went to Paris, where, we are told, he became so enamoured of French manners, customs, and fashions, that on his return to England he could speak and boast of nothing else. Handsome, well-born, and accomplished, he soon attracted the notice of Henry the Eighth, who welcomed him at Court, and appointed him a Gentleman of the Privy Chamber, a place which was then of much higher standing than in later days. But Carew did not make himself popular in the royal household. The constant comparisons which he daily drew between the French and English Courts, to the great disparagement of the latter, offended his colleagues in the highest degree, and were not calculated to gratify the King. Henry resolved to give the young man a lesson. If he were so devoted to France, to France he should go, and that without delay. At the same time, unwilling to dismiss him without some ostensible reason, he appointed Sir Nicholas governor of a fortress in Picardy, which was in the hands of the English. A castle in a provincial town did not offer the charms which Carew had found in the splendid capital of France, and it may easily be believed the office did not suit his taste. He doubtless petitioned the King; at all events, he was recalled, forgiven, and taken back into favour. He now became Henry's almost inseparable companion, and was foremost in all the jousts, tournaments, maskings, and all kinds of Court revelry, in which they both excelled and delighted. Carew was, moreover, appointed Master of the Horse, at that period one of the highest offices in the realm, and Knight of the Garter.

The favour of Henry the Eighth was as easily lost as won, and Fuller tells us that a tradition in the family reported that Carew's downfall proceeded, in the first instance, from a quarrel between him and his master at bowls, 'when his Grace, who was no good fellow, and would always rather give than take in repartee,' so exasperated his Master of the Horse, 'that his answer was rather true than discreet, consulting his own animosity rather than his allegiance, whereat the King was so offended that Sir Nicholas fell from the top of his favour to the bottom of his displeasure, and was bruised to death.' 'This'—we quote Fuller all the time—'was the true cause of his execution. He was charged with high treason, as accomplice with the Marquis of Exeter, Lord Montague, Sir Edward Neville, and others, in a plot to depose King Henry the Eighth, and place Cardinal Pole on the throne. They were all found guilty, and sentenced to death, with the exception of the Cardinal's brother, who saved his own life by betraying his confederates. The evidence against Sir Nicholas appears to have been slight, but he was out of favour, and everything was turned to his prejudice. He was beheaded on Tower Hill in 1539.' Holinshed said 'he made a godly confession of his fault, and his superstitious faith.' He was a Roman Catholic. Sir Nicholas Carew married Elizabeth, daughter and afterwards sole heir of Sir Thomas Bryan, Master of Common Pleas, by whom he had one son and three or four daughters.

The son, Sir Francis Carew, never married, but having regained a considerable portion of the estates forfeited on his father's attainder, during the reign of Elizabeth, he bequeathed his property to his sister's son, Sir Nicholas Throckmorton, on condition that he assumed the name and arms of Carew.

No. 27.   AN OLD MAN'S HEAD.

BY VANDYCK.

No. 28.   MAN'S HEAD.

BY TINTORETTO.

No. 30. THE COUNTESS OF OXFORD.

Blue and white dress. Holding a nosegay. A table beside her.

BY VANDYCK.

BEATRIX VAN HEMMEND, a Dutch lady, a native of Friesland, married Robert de Vere, nineteenth Earl of Oxford. He died in 1632, at the siege of Maestricht, leaving an only surviving child, in whom the earldom became extinct.

No. 33. PORTRAIT. UNKNOWN.

BY TITIAN.

No. 36. SIR KENELM DIGBY.

Black dress. Hand on his breast. A globe by his side.

BORN 1603, DIED 1665.

BY VANDYCK.

SON of Sir Everard Digby, born at Gothurst or Gayhurst, County Bucks, the property of his mother, daughter and sole heir of Sir William Mulsho. He was but a child when his father suffered death as one of the conspirators in the Gunpowder Plot. The Crown laid claim to the estates and revenues of the family; but the widowed Lady Digby, a woman of great energy and determination, not only saved her own dower by her strenuous efforts, but rescued a few hundreds for her son out of the wreck, and, although a rigid Roman Catholic, she suffered her boy to be educated as a Protestant from prudential motives. The romance of the loves of Kenelm Digby and Venetia Stanley, which made such a noise at the time, and has been the subject of curiosity and controversy ever since, whenever their names are mentioned, began at a very early age. Sir Edward Stanley, of the noble house of Derby, lived at Tong Castle, County Salop. He married the daughter and co-heir of the Earl of Northumberland, who brought him two daughters, 'the divine Venetia' being the youngest. Her mother died when she was a few months old. The widower gave himself up to grief, shunned the world, and could not even derive comfort from the society of his children. He sent them therefore (or at all events Venetia) to the care of a relative, who was a neighbour of Lady Digby's. Thus began the acquaintance, and Sir Edward's beautiful little girl and Lady Digby's lovely boy met constantly, and played at love-making, jealousy, rivalry, coquetry, quarrels, reconciliations,— in fact a perfect rehearsal of all the drama that was to be enacted in good earnest a few years later. The marriage of the Princess Elizabeth with the Elector Palatine, afterwards King of Bohemia, called Sir Edward to London. With a violent wrench he tore himself away from his seclusion, and sending for Venetia carried her with him to the Court of King James, then the scene of great festivity.

In all these gaieties, according to Digby's account, the juvenile beauty took part, and was the centre of admiration. In the meantime her young lover pursued his studies under the care of Laud, Dean of Gloucester, subsequently Archbishop of Canterbury, and afterwards with Dr. Thomas Allen, an eminent scholar, at Oxford.

Digby distinguished himself at the University, where he remained two years, but whenever he returned home for the vacation, the flirtation with his fair neighbour was resumed. He wrote a strange and wild romance respecting her, in which it is impossible to disentangle truth from fiction, but some of the adventures are too marvellous for belief, and the whole narrative is disagreeable, and tedious into the bargain.

His jealousy seems to have been excited by a certain courtier, whose suit, he affirms, was favoured by Venetia's governess. Lady Digby was too wise a mother to smile on such a precocious courtship, even if she disbelieved the reports which had already begun to circulate, detrimental to Mistress Stanley's reputation.

She despatched her son on foreign travel, but before his departure the lovers had met and plighted their troth. According to the traveller's own account, he made a conquest of the French Queen when in Paris *en route* for Italy.

A report of his death having been accidentally or purposely circulated, Venetia's conduct on the occasion was differently represented to her absent lover, some declaring she was inconsolable, others that she lent a willing ear to the suit of the very same courtier who had before excited Kenelm's jealousy.

Nothing can be more bombastic and high-flown than the language in which he describes the fluctuations of his passion for Venetia, his implicit trust in her constancy in one page, his doubts and suspicions in another.

It seems more than probable that the prudent Lady Digby intercepted her son's love-letters, and did all in her power to prevent a marriage she thought most undesirable, and she was doubtless delighted when Kenelm accompanied his kinsman, Lord Bristol, to Spain, where he was then negotiating the Prince of Wales's marriage with the Infanta at Madrid. Kenelm became himself attached to the Prince's suite, and took an active part in diplomatic transactions.

In this land of romance it may well be imagined that the handsome and accomplished Englishman ran the gauntlet of many adventures among the dark-eyed daughters of the South, nor does he omit to allude to innumerable conquests; indeed, he went so far as to have a portrait of himself painted with an effigy of one of his victims in the background, yet he incessantly boasted of his constancy to the absent loved one. On his return to England with the Prince of Wales, he was knighted by the King at Hinchingbrook, and immediately flew to his lady-love in spite of maternal prohibition. Then followed recriminations, explanations, trials of her faith and virtue, challenges, duels—a stormy suit, indeed, according to his own testimony.

Respecting the date of their marriage there is great difference of opinion. At all events, Kenelm insisted on its being kept secret, nor was poor Venetia allowed to announce it, even when a fall from her horse brought on a premature confinement, which nearly cost her her life.

King James admired Sir Kenelm for his great erudition, and complimented him on his essays on Sympathetic Powder, Alchemy, and other subjects bordering on the supernatural. On the accession of Charles the First, Sir Kenelm Digby was made Gentleman of the Privy Chamber, Commissioner of the Navy, and Governor of the Trinity House, shortly after which, he was appointed to the command of a naval squadron, sent to the Mediterranean against the Venetian fleet and the Algerine pirates.

In this voyage he was eminently successful, bringing the Venetians to terms, chastising the pirates, and releasing a large number of English slaves. It is said that on the eve of his embarkation, a second son being born to him, he had permitted his wife to declare their marriage, and had consigned her to the care of his kinsman, Lord Bristol, during his absence from England. About this time, his faithful old friend, Thomas Allen, bequeathed to him a splendid library, which he made over to the Bodleian.

In 1633, after his return, his beautiful but far from happy wife died, and the mystery which had shrouded Venetia's whole life hung like a dark cloud over her death, and reports of all kinds were current.

There is no doubt that Sir Kenelm had been in the habit of making chemical and alchemical experiments on Venetia for some time past, and the tradition of the concoction of snails which he had invented as a preservative of her naturally brilliant complexion is still extant at Gayhurst, where it is said the somewhat rare breed of large 'Pomatia' is still to be found.

By Digby's desire his wife's head ('which contained but little brain') was opened, and he decided that she had taken an overdose of viper wine. But spiteful women declared she had fallen a victim to a viper husband's jealousy, though Aubrey, who tells sad tales of Venetia before her marriage, says she was a blameless wife.

There is more than one portrait of her, with allegorical emblems of Innocence, Slander, and the like. Her name had often been coupled with that of the Earl of Dorset, and some said he had settled an annuity on her, which was paid up to the time of her death. Be this as it may, Sir Kenelm and Lady Digby always dined once a year with my Lord Dorset, who received them courteously but formally, only permitting himself to kiss the beauty's hand with great respect.

Venetia was buried in a church near Newgate, in a tomb of black marble, with long inscriptions, surmounted by a copper-gilt bust, all destroyed in the great fire. Numerous epitaphs were written in her honour. Ben Jonson calls her 'A tender mother, a discreet wife, a solemn mistress, a good friend, so lovely and charitable in all her petite actions, so devote in her whole life,' etc.

Whatever Sir Kenelm's real feelings were, his outward grief was extreme. He retired to Gresham College, lived like a hermit, studied chemistry, wore a long mourning cloak, and

T

left his beard unshorn. Although it was generally supposed that his secession from the Protestant faith took place when he was in Spain, it was not until 1653 that he wrote to his friend Laud (whose admirable answer is extant) to announce the fact. He was a firm adherent of Charles I., and greatly esteemed by Henrietta Maria; but his loyalty got him into trouble with the Parliament, and he was exiled to France. Returning in a few months he was imprisoned in 1640 for nearly three years, and was supposed only to have regained his liberty through the intercession of the French Queen, who had loved him twenty years before. His release, however, was conditional. He was forbidden to take part in any public affairs, and he therefore gave himself up to literary and scientific pursuits, and engaged in a polemical correspondence with his quondam tutor, Laud, whom he is said to have tempted to change his faith, by the bait of a Cardinal's Hat. Sir Kenelm returned to France and frequented the Court of his old flame, the Queen Dowager, where his noble appearance, almost gigantic size, his handsome features, agreeable conversation and manners, his learning, and last, but perhaps not least, his predilection for the occult sciences, made him an universal favourite. On the death of his eldest son, killed on the Royalist side at the battle of St. Neot's, Sir Kenelm returned to compound for his estates, but was not suffered to remain in England. He went back to Paris, where Henrietta Maria made him her Chancellor; and he was then intrusted with a mission to Pope Innocent X., who welcomed him at first, but after a time the 'Englishman grew high, and hectored at His Holiness, and gave him the lie.'

Once more in England, after the dissolution of the Long Parliament, Cromwell took him into his confidence, hoping by his mediation to gain over the Roman Catholics.

His conduct in these circumstances has been praised by some and censured by others, as may well be imagined, according to religious and political bias. He travelled through France, Lower Germany, and the Palatinate, always seeking and being sought by men of letters; and 1660 saw him once more back in his native land.

Charles II. showed him but little favour. He was nominated F.R.S., and resided (1663) in a fair house in Covent Garden, where he had a laboratory. 'Philosopher, theologian, courtier, soldier; polite, amiable, handsome, graceful.' Lord Clarendon's testimony is, 'eccentric, vain, unstable in religion, a duellist.' These are the counterbalancing portraits of Sir Kenelm Digby. He desired to be buried near Venetia. His epitaph was as follows :—

> 'Under this tomb the matchless Digby lies,
> Digby the great, the brilliant, and the wise ;
> This age's wonder, for his noble partes,
> Skilled in six tongues, and learn'd in all the artes !
> Born on the day he died, th' eleventh of June,
> And that day bravely fought at Scanderoon :
> It's rare that one and the same day should be
> The day of birth, and death, and victory.'

He had four sons and one daughter.

No. 40.   SIR THOMAS KILLIGREW.

Red slashed doublet.   Fair hair.   A bracelet on his arm.   His hand rests on a dog's head.

BORN 1611, DIED 1683.

BY VANDYCK.

E was the younger son of Sir Robert Killigrew of Hanworth, County Middlesex, by Mary, daughter of Sir Henry Wodehouse, who married, secondly, Sir Thomas Stafford. Thomas, or as he was usually called, Tom Killigrew, was early initiated into the mysteries of Court life, being appointed Page of Honour to King Charles the First, to whom he remained faithful, and followed Charles the Second and his mother in their exile. About the year 1651 the King sent him in a diplomatic capacity to Venice, where Killigrew seems to have disported himself to his heart's content, and it was evidently here that he imbibed that passion for music and the drama, which never forsook him, but which converted him into a dramatist and a theatrical *entrepreneur*, rather, we should say, confirmed him in these tastes which were already developed in his boyhood; for we have an anecdote of his school days, how he would go to the Red Bull Tavern, not far from the theatre, during the performance, and how, more than once, the waiter came in crying, 'Who will go and be a devil on the stage, and he shall see the play for nothing?' an offer with which young Tom gladly closed. Thus began his career; for was not he a merry devil the chief part of his life?

Venice, as we have seen, suited his humour well, and Thomas was evidently one of those foreigners who go on the principle of howling with the wolves, and doing at Rome more than the Romans do. In fact, he was so carried away by the vivacity of the Venetians, the maskings, flirtings, and what not, which he encountered in the fair city of the sea, that Thomas began to out-Herod Herod, and lived his life at such a rate as to scandalise the Venetian authorities, who directed their ambassador at Paris to wait on the English King, and urge the recall of his envoy. Charles complied, but it was not likely that the peccadilloes of which 'Tommaso' had been guilty should appear unpardonable in the eyes of the merry monarch, and he received the delinquent into especial favour, and on the Restoration Tom became Groom of the Bedchamber, and the King's inseparable companion. Pepys, in his diary of 1660, about the time of Charles's return to his dominions, records his meeting with Tom, when being on my Lord Sandwich's ship, he met, 'with other fine company, Tom Killigrew, a merry droll, but a gentleman, full of wit and humour, a general favourite, especially with the King. And I walked with him for some time on the deck, and he told most amusing stories.'

Killigrew had not been long in England before he put a darling scheme into execution, namely, to bring over an Italian troop of actors from Venice to perform in singing and recitative. He had by this time set up as a dramatic author, and was instrumental in introducing into England the fashion of female performers, for, until the Restoration, actresses had not appeared on the stage, although in Italy, Spain, and elsewhere, the female characters were always represented by women. It may easily be believed that this innovation fell in with the royal taste, and there was great amusement afforded by a representation of the Parson's Wedding, a comedy of Master Killigrew's own writing, entirely performed by females. In another portion of his diary Pepys relates how he met Tom at my Lord Brouncker's one night in company with a certain musician, one Signor Baptista, and Killigrew told us how they proposed to give an opera entirely in the Italian language, and he goes on to say that Baptista was singer, poet, and all in one, and that he sang them one of the acts, and that from the words alone, without any music prickt, which seemed to astonish good Master Samuel, who makes some of his accustomed sapient remarks on the occasion: 'I did not understand the words, and so do not know if they are fitted, but I perceive there is a proper accent in every country's discourse, but I am not as much smitten by it as if I were acquainted with the language.'

Good Master Pepys had made a discovery in those early times, which we recommend to the notice of many who pass in these days for proficients in the vocal line. The newly-born Italian opera now became the rage, very often, indeed, to the detriment of the English theatrical companies, so much so that sometimes Killigrew's own dramatic productions were played to empty benches. Besides Signor Baptista there was another eminent musician, Francesco Corbetta, who not only sang in opera, but gave lessons in singing and the guitar, an instrument hitherto almost unknown in this country.

> 'Famossissimo maestro, di ghitarra,
> Qual Orfeo in suonar, ognun il narra!'

Guitar-playing became a perfect mania among the fine ladies and gentlemen at Court, 'the King's relish for that instrument,' says De Grammont, 'helping to bring it into vogue, and the guitar (whether for show or use) was now as necessary an appendage to a lady's toilet-table as her rouge or patch-box. In fact, there was a universal strumming of the whole *guitarrery* at Court.' Lord Arran, a younger son of the Duke of Ormonde, and his sister were amongst the greatest proficients; indeed, Lady Chesterfield was as much admired for her musical talent as for her undoubted beauty, and it was whispered her lord was very jealous of the Duke of York's evident appreciation of both these attractions. Tom Killigrew's popularity with the King increased daily, and there was a report that his Majesty intended to revive the disused office of Court Jester in the person of his favourite. We believe such an *officer* had been attached to his father's household, but the post could only have been nominal. An old writer thus describes the duties of a Court Jester, 'A witty and jocose person kept by princes, to inform them of their faults, and those of other people.' We scarcely give Charles the Second credit for such a motive in his election. Pepys alludes to the circumstance in these words, 'Tom Killigrew has a fee out of the Wardrobe for Cap and Bells as King's Jester, and may tease and rule anybody, the greatest person, without offence, in privilege of his place.' Of this privilege Tom took advantage, sometimes in a good cause, for with all their faults and failings, both he and his kindred spirit, Nell Gwynne, regretted the bad odour into which Charles had fallen through his neglect of public affairs, and Nell often admonished her royal lover on the subject. One day the two friends hatched a small plot. Says Nelly, 'I have been just listening to the complaints of one of the Court Lords, of Charles's neglect of all duty, and how that he has quite forgotten the existence of such a thing as a Cabinet Council, upon which I bet his Lordship £100 that the King should attend the very next. He sneered, but accepted the wager.' Now we do not know if Nelly promised her accomplice to go halves, but we do know that that evening, when the King was in Madam Gwynne's apartments, the door flew open, and in burst Tom, disguised as a pilgrim. The King swore at him, and asked if he had not heard the royal command that he should not be disturbed. 'Oh yes, sire,' was the reply, 'but I was obliged to come and take leave of your Majesty before my departure.'

'Why, where the —— are you going, and what does this absurd masquerading mean?'

'I am starting this very moment for hell.'

'Already,' sneered the King, 'and on what errand?'

'To beg and pray of the devil to lend me Oliver Cromwell, if for ever so short a time, to attend to the affairs of the country, as his successor spends all his time in pleasure.'

The Jester was forgiven, and Nelly won her wager.

Another time Charles taxed his fool with telling everybody that the King was suffering from torturing pains in the nose, and asked the meaning of such a senseless report. 'I crave your Majesty's pardon,' says Tom, 'I knew you had been led by the nose for so many years, that I felt sure it must have become tender and painful.'

But the Jester occasionally carried the jest too far; there was a play called 'The Silent Woman,' given in London about this time, wherein appeared the character of Tom Otter, a henpecked husband, a reputation which the Duke of York enjoyed at Court. One night Charles said, 'I will go no more abroad with Tom Otter and his wife.' Now the courtiers well knew that when the King made any slighting allusion to his brother, they were expected to be tickled, so there was a general roar. The Jester alone looked solemn. 'I wonder,' said he, 'which is best, to play Tom Otter to your wife or to your mistress?'—a sally which made Charles very angry, for he felt the reference was made to Lady Castlemaine, of whom the whole world knew he stood greatly in awe.

Another evening Tom made a comic onslaught on Lord Rochester, and that nobleman, actuated perhaps by *jalousie de métier*, was so enraged that he dealt the Jester a swinging box on the ear, unmindful of the royal presence, and threw the whole Court circle into confusion.

Death alone could put an end to poor Tom's fooling. He died at his post at Whitehall in 1682-3, and then 'where were his gibes, his gambols, his flashes of merriment, that were wont to set the table in a roar? Alas! poor Yorick.'

Dining-Room.

No. 43.   MISTRESS HERBERT.

Elizabethan dress. Ruff. Jewelled hat. Auburn hair. Inscription—
'*Richard Herbert of Blackhall's wife, being daughter to Newport of Arcole.*'

DIED 1627.

BY ZUCCHERO.

E cannot do better in giving an account of this most remarkable and exemplary woman than to quote the words of her distinguished son, Edward, ~~tenth~~ Lord Herbert of Cherbury: 'My mother, Magdalen, was the fourth daughter of Sir Richard Newport, by his wife, Margaret, daughter and heir of Sir Thomas Bromley, one of the Privy Council, and Executor of King Henry the Eighth. She married Richard Herbert, grandson of Sir Richard Herbert of Blackhall, County Montgomery, Knight, and surviving her husband, gave rare testimonies of an incomparable piety to God and love to her children. She was most assiduous and devout in her daily, both private and public, prayers, and so careful to provide for her posterity, that though it were in her power to give her estate, which was very great, to whom she would, yet she continued long unmarried, and so provident for them, that after she had bestowed all her daughters with sufficient portions upon very good neighbouring families she delivered up her estate and care of her housekeeping to her eldest son Francis. She had for many years kept hospitality with that plenty and order as exceeded all, either of her county or town, for besides abundance of provision and good cheer for guests, which her son Sir Francis continued, she used ever after dinner to distribute with her own hands to the poor, who resorted to her in great numbers. Alms in money she gave also, more or less, as she thought they needed it. After my mother had lived most virtuously and lovingly with her husband for many years (who died in 1597), she after his death erected a fair monument for him in Montgomery Church, brought up her children carefully, and put them in good courses for making their fortunes, and briefly was that woman Dr. Donne has described in his funeral sermon.'

Speaking of his father Lord Herbert says : 'He was blackhaired, and bearded, of a manly but somewhat stern look, but withal very handsome; compact in his limbs, and of a great courage.' His grandfather was also distinguished for the same quality, and was noted to be a great enemy to the outlaws and thieves of his time, who appeared in great numbers in the mountains of Montgomeryshire. Lord Herbert also commends his grandfather's extreme hospitality, which caused it to be an ordinary saying, if any one saw a fowl rise in the country at that time—' Fly where thou wilt, thou wilt light at Blackhall.'

Mistress Herbert had seven sons, of whom the eldest was the aforementioned Lord Herbert of Cherbury, and three daughters. She seems to have merited her son's encomiums. Izaak Walton says of her : 'She was a person of superior abilities, and was highly esteemed for her great and harmless wit, cheerful gaiety, and obliging behaviour, which gained her a friendship with most of any eminent birth or learning in the University of Oxford, where she resided four years during the time of her widowhood, in order to superintend the education of her children, who were all young at the time of their father's death. When she had provided for them she took to her second husband, Sir John Danvers, Knight, brother and heir to Henry, Earl of Danby, who highly valued both her person and most excellent endowments of mind. It was Magdalen Newport, Mrs. Herbert, and Dame Danvers, who inspired those favourite lines of Dr. Donne, Dean of St. Paul's, so often quoted—

> ' No spring or summer beauty hath such grace
> As I have seen in an autumnal face.'

She lies buried at Chelsea.

No. 44.

THOMAS CROMWELL, EARL OF ESSEX.

Black and white dress.

BY HOLBEIN.

E was the son of a blacksmith at Putney; his mother, who married again, sent him to a small school, where he learned little more than reading, writing, and the rudiments of Latin. When quite young he evinced a passion for travel, and set out for the Continent with very scanty means, which were soon exhausted, and he found himself at Antwerp without money or connections of any kind. But he was energetic and hardworking, and he soon found employment as a clerk in an English factory established in the city. Glad as Cromwell was to earn his livelihood, the drudgery and confinement of the life were irksome to the eager restless spirit of our young adventurer, and he took advantage of the first opportunity to escape. He made acquaintance with some countrymen from Boston in Lincolnshire, bound for Rome, in order to obtain certain indulgences from the reigning Pope, Julius the Second. These men soon became aware that Cromwell's intelligence and capability were likely to make him a valuable fellow-traveller. They therefore proposed to convey him to Italy, an offer with which it may be imagined Cromwell eagerly closed. At Rome he rose into favour at the Vatican by his talent and ability, added to which substantial qualifications our young traveller made himself acceptable to the Pope by ministering to the well-known tastes of Julius for good living. He is said to have instructed the Papal cook in the art of preparing many a delicacy for the Pontiff's table, till then unknown in Rome, especially '*some rare English jellies, which his Holiness pronounced delicious.*' Italy was at that period the theatre of constant warfare, and Cromwell became not only a spectator, but an actor in many of the exciting events, serving for a time as trooper in the army of the Duke, afterwards Connétable, de Bourbon.

This great commander had left the service of France in disgust, and had espoused the cause of Charles the Fifth, Emperor of Germany. A companion in arms was John Russell, eventually Earl of Bedford; a man who shone alike as a soldier and a diplomatist, and had been employed in the latter capacity by Henry the Eighth, and his prime minister, Cardinal Wolsey. Being at Bologna a plot was formed to seize his person and send him prisoner to Paris, the hotel in which he lodged being already guarded by the soldiers of the Gonfaloniere. Thomas Cromwell was also in Bologna at that time, and no sooner did he receive intelligence of the affair than he went to the municipal authorities representing himself as a Neapolitan acquaintance of the English knight, and offering to persuade him to give himself up quietly. He thus gained access to Russell's presence, and providing him with the disguise of a peasant contrived in the most skilful manner to effect his escape. Russell urged his deliverer to accompany him, but Cromwell was not disposed to leave Italy so soon, and entered the service of a rich merchant at Venice. Cromwell was said to have been present at the battle of Pavia, where Francis the First of France was taken prisoner. On his return to England, the man whose life and liberty he had saved, came forward to lend him a helping hand.

Russell, then in much repute at Court, recommended him to the patronage of Wolsey, then in the zenith of his power. The Cardinal took Cromwell into his service and confidence, and made him secretary and chief agent in the great scheme of the dissolution of the religious houses, which was now carrying on, the funds thus raised being ostensibly apportioned to defraying the expenses attendant on the erection of the colleges which Wolsey was now founding—

> 'Those twin seats of learning,
> Ipswich and Oxford.'

But there were whisperings abroad that much of the money thus obtained overflowed into the pockets of 'master and man,' a circumstance which Cromwell emphatically denied in a conversation with Master George Cavendish, one of the Cardinal's gentlemen, and his eventual biographer. The question of Cromwell's fidelity to his master, when Wolsey fell on evil days, has been differently treated by different writers; but there is no doubt that when Wolsey left London in disgrace, Cromwell followed him to Esher—or Asher, as it is written by Master Cavendish—who tells us he went into the great chamber, and to his surprise found Master Cromwell standing in the large window, the tears distilling from his eyes, with a primer in his hand, praying earnestly,—'the which was a strange sight,' for it did not appear that the said Master Cromwell was by any means given to devotion. Cavendish inquired into the cause of his sorrow, asking anxiously if he considered their master's case to be so very hopeless, on which Cromwell, with much candour, confessed that it was his own fate he was bewailing, for it seemed most likely that he was on the point of losing everything for which he had been travailing all the days of his life; moreover, that he was in disdain of all men simply for doing his master's service, through which he had never increased his living, on the contrary, had been a heavy loser. Then he confided to Master Cavendish how, that very afternoon, when the Cardinal had dined, it was his (Cromwell's) intention to ride with all speed to London, and so to Court, 'where I will either make or mar ere I come back again.' Assuredly in the audience which he solicited and obtained did Master Cromwell make, and not mar, as far as he himself was concerned. He had a long and explicit conversation with the King, into whose favour he ingratiated himself by suggesting the very line of conduct on which he well knew Henry's heart was bent. Acquainted with the Monarch's infatuation for Anne Boleyn, he now suggested, as if from his own notion of advisability, that the King should throw off all allegiance to the Pope, declare himself supreme head of the Church throughout his own kingdom, and thus facilitate the much desired measure of his divorce from Queen Katherine. Such palatable advice was indeed well calculated to win Henry's good graces, and from that moment Cromwell's rapid rise began. The King, knowing what a valuable auxiliary he had proved to his late patron in the matter of the suppression of the religious houses, resolved to secure Cromwell's services for the same purpose. He therefore confirmed him in the office of Steward of the Dissolved Monasteries, made him a Privy Councillor, a Knight, Secretary of State, Master of the Royal Jewel-house, Clerk of the Hanaper (a lucrative post in the Court of Chancery), and what Cromwell's enemies termed 'the Lord knows what.' In 1535 Visitor-General of the said suppressed monasteries throughout the realm, in which capacity Sir Thomas incurred much censure, and was branded by many as cruel, rapacious, and overbearing. In our judgment of this sentence we must take into consideration the fever heat at which religious animosity now stood; suffice it to say that Cromwell satisfied the views of his royal master, and was not Henry cruel, rapacious, and overbearing? Fabulous sums were extorted from the exchequers of these establishments, and it was almost universally believed that the favourite came in for a considerable share of the booty. It was indeed evident he did not remember the injunction laid upon him by Sir Thomas More, namely, that he should advise the King what he *ought* to do, not only what he was *able* to do. In 1536 he was made Privy Seal, and the same year Baron Cromwell of Okeham, County Rutland, and (the authority of the Pope being by this time abolished in England) Henry instituted a new office, to which he appointed his favourite. This was Vicar-General, or in other words, Supreme Head of the Church, as representative of the King, in which capacity he sat in the House of Lords, and also at Convocation above the Archbishop of Canterbury. The office included that of Principal Commissary for the Administration of Justice in all ecclesiastical affairs; of the godly reformation, and the redress of all errors, heresies, and abuses of the English Reformed Church, both in Parliament and Convocation.

It was indeed strange that the man who, a very short time before, had professed infidel doctrines (and was so unsettled in his creed that when Cavendish found him at prayers, the primer in his hand should be our lady's matins) strange to say that this individual should now come forward as the principal pillar of the Reformation. Dr. Hook, in his *Lives of the Archbishops of Canterbury*, says, Cromwell 'was not a real Protestant, and was generally supposed to be a man who supported the party from which he could obtain most, a statesman whose religion depended on politics, and who had no knowledge of theological subjects.' Yet from the circumstances in which he was now placed all the English Protestants rallied round him, and those of Germany treated with him. In his new capacity Cromwell issued the most stringent and binding regulations for the conduct of the reformed clergy, was indefatigable in propagating the Bible throughout the country, causing it to be read in churches, and placed in convenient parts of the building, where the parishioners themselves could refer to it on their own account. But Cromwell's life forms part of the history of the reign of Henry the Eighth, and indeed of the Reformation itself. And it is incumbent on us to condense this narrative lest it exceed the prescribed bounds.

He continued to receive marks of favour from the King, but his keen eye detected the gathering clouds in his own future; and he knew if Henry once failed him there would be little hope of stemming the tide of unpopularity which threatened to overpower him. He well knew that he was hated by all classes; the nobility, who grudged all the titles and honours bestowed on 'the blacksmith's son'; the Roman Catholics, who had good reason to detest him; while the reformed clergy rebelled against many of the changes and innovations which the Vicar-General had instituted in the services and conduct of the Church; and the poorer classes were indignant with him for depriving them of the bounty which they had so long received from the religious houses. Cromwell had good cause to be uneasy. He began by propitiating 'the poor and needy,' who now flocked by invitation to the gate of his house in Throckmorton Street, oftentimes twice a day, where they were regaled with bread and meat and money. He then set on foot negotiations with the Protestant Princes of Germany, more especially the reigning Duke of Cleves, in order to bring about a marriage between that Prince's sister and Henry the Eighth, who was at this moment in one of his transitory intervals of widowhood. Lord Cromwell imagined that a Protestant queen of his own selection would be an invaluable ally at Court, and help him to retain the favour of the King, who was persuaded into the belief that the

Lady Anne of Cleves was not only 'fair and portly,' but comely in face and feature, an error in which Henry was confirmed by a very flattering portrait from the pencil of Holbein. So the Princess was sent for to come over to England, and a magnificent cortége was despatched, with the Archbishop of Canterbury himself, to bring her on her way to London; and Henry conceived the romantic idea of riding down to Rochester in disguise to waylay his bride. Alas! for the eager glance which his Grace cast into the travelling coach, where sat a lady tall and portly indeed, but coarse and ugly in face and feature! Henry, we are told, was 'alarmed and abashed,' but he also was furious. He felt he had been deceived, and he sent for Cromwell and bade him devise some means for the prevention of the marriage. It was too late; matters had gone too far, and the ceremony was performed.

It would appear that at the time the King did not realise the idea that Cromwell was the principal instigator of the hated union, for it was after the marriage that he was raised to the Earldom of Essex, and made Lord Chamberlain, and his son granted a separate peerage. We know from the pages of history how the King's horror of 'the Flanders mare' increased day by day, and he never rested till he had obtained a divorce, soon followed by the downfall of the newly created Earl of Essex, whose ruin was resolved on.

The Duke of Norfolk was intrusted with the task of arresting his enemy at the Council Board on the opening of Parliament in June 1540, and despatching him to the Tower, nor was he loth to carry out the royal command. Essex claimed a trial by his Peers, but the privilege was denied him. He was condemned, says Dr. Hook, by the iniquitous statute, admitting of attainder without trial, a measure of which he was not the actual founder, as affirmed by some writers, but the reviver of the same, and therefore by many pronounced deserving of his fate.

He was accused of high treason, heresy, embezzlement, and a host of other misdemeanours, but there is little doubt the worst offence in Henry's eyes was his instrumentality in promoting the hateful marriage with Anne of Cleves.

The only voice that was raised in his behalf was that of Archbishop Cranmer, who wrote a most eloquent letter to the King, entreating him to spare the life of Lord Essex, but it was unavailing. Cromwell's demeanour in the Tower was very different from that which had characterised Sir Thomas More. He addressed the most abject letters to Henry, and would have accepted life at almost any price. He wrote 'with a heavy heart and trembling hand,' and signed himself, 'Your highness's most humble and wretched prisoner and poor slave, Thomas Cromwell.' While underneath the subscription came the words, 'I cry for mercy, mercy, mercy!'

Henry caused the letters to be read to him four times, and at one moment showed signs of relenting, but in the end was (as usual) inexorable. Four days from the passing of the sentence, Lord Essex was led forth to execution, and beheaded on Tower Hill. He made a speech full of loyalty and submission to the royal will, words which were thought to have been dictated by paternal solicitude for the welfare of his only son. He furthermore confessed his sins, repenting that he had ever abandoned the Catholic faith to which he now returned, for in that he was resolved to die; then kneeling in prayer, 'he submitted his neck to the executioner, who mangled him in a shocking manner.'

No. 46. **LADY KILLIGREW.**

Standing. White satin gown, dark drapery. Hands crossed. Brown curls.

BY VANDYCK.

MISTRESS Cecilia Crofts, maid of honour to the Queen Henrietta Maria?

PRINCIPAL STAIRCASE.

PRINCIPAL STAIRCASE.

No. 1. GRACE, COUNTESS OF DYSART.

Pale yellow dress. Leaning her elbow on a table.

DIED 1744.

BY WRIGHT.

HE was the daughter of Sir Thomas Wilbraham of Woodhey, County Chester, by Elizabeth, daughter and sole heir of Edward Mytton, Esq., of Weston-under-Lizard, County Stafford. She married, 1680, Lionel Tollemache, Earl of Dysart, and, becoming co-heir with her sister, the Countess of Bradford, took large estates to her husband's family. Lady Dysart had one son, who died *v.p.*, and two daughters.

No. 2.
MARY, WIFE OF RICHARD NEWPORT, SECOND EARL OF BRADFORD.

Pale yellow dress. Pink drapery. Holding a flower.

BORN 1661, DIED 1737.

BY WRIGHT.

HE was the daughter and co-heir of Sir Thomas Wilbraham of Woodhey, County Chester, Bart., by Elizabeth, daughter and co-heir of Edward Mytton, Esq. of Weston-under-Lizard, which estate (besides a large fortune from her father) Lady Bradford inherited from her mother, and brought into the Newport family.

It is seldom the lot of any woman to live continuously in one loved home, but Mary Wilbraham was born, married, died, and was buried at Weston, where her childhood, youth, the chief part of her married life, and the latter days of her widowhood were all passed, and which she brought into the Newport family. Francis, Earl of Bradford, and his wife were most anxious to secure for their eldest son so desirable a match as this young lady presented, not only on account of her noble inheritance, but in respect of her amiable qualities and the comeliness of her person.

They accordingly made good settlements on Lord Newport to facilitate the union. We have a list of the lands and messuages allotted to him, but to prove their worth we consider two of them will suffice, at least in point of syllables, namely— the Manors of Ginnioneth-ys-Kerdine, and Dykewyde, in the county of Cardigan. Lady Bradford had six sons, of whom four died without children, and two, Henry and Thomas, succeeded to the Earldom, and four daughters, Mary, who died unmarried; Elizabeth, wife of James Cocks of Worcester, Esq., ancestor to the present Lord Somers; Anne, married to Sir Orlando Bridgeman of Castle Bromwich, County Warwick, Bart.; and Diana, married to Algernon Coote, Earl of Mountrath. Mary, Countess of Bradford, survived her husband many years, and lies buried by his side at Weston. Her loss was deeply mourned by all classes, especially by the poor, to whom her charity was unbounded.

No. 3. RICHARD NEWPORT, SECOND EARL OF BRADFORD.

Slashed dress of golden brown. White sleeves. Wig.

BORN 1644, DIED 1723.

BY SIR PETER LELY.

E was the eldest son of the first Earl of Bradford, by Lady Diana Russell. During his father's lifetime he represented Shropshire in Parliament for many years, and gained great popularity in his county by his strenuous support of the Bill of Exclusion, which obtained for him a complimentary address signed by every member of the grand jury, consisting of all the principal landholders of the neighbourhood. He was Privy Councillor in the reigns of Queen Anne and George the First, and Lord Lieutenant and *Custos Rotulorum* for the county of Montgomery. In 1681 he married the daughter and co-heir of Sir Thomas Wilbraham of Woodhey, and Weston-under-Lizard, Bart., by whom he had a numerous family. During his father's lifetime he resided chiefly at Eyton-upon-Severn, but in later days he took up his abode at Weston, his wife's inheritance in Staffordshire.

No. 4.

SIR ORLANDO BRIDGEMAN.

Robes of the Lord-Keeper. Holding the purse. Oval, in a square frame.

BORN 1609, DIED 1674.

BY RILEY.

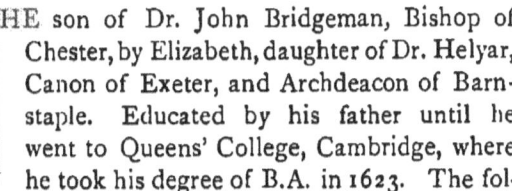

HE son of Dr. John Bridgeman, Bishop of Chester, by Elizabeth, daughter of Dr. Helyar, Canon of Exeter, and Archdeacon of Barnstaple. Educated by his father until he went to Queens' College, Cambridge, where he took his degree of B.A. in 1623. The following year he entered the Inner Temple, and applied himself vigorously to the study of common law, 'of which he became,' says Lord Campbell, 'a profound master, caring little in comparison for either literature or politics.' When called to the bar he made himself remarkable for his diligent attention to business, although he had the expectation of a goodly inheritance from his father. At the commencement of the Long Parliament Orlando Bridgeman was returned for the borough of Wigan in Lancashire. He voted silently, but, with the exception of some measures on which he had conscientious scruples, almost invariably for the King. He was also one of the few who voted against the attainder of Lord Strafford, in whose behalf he made a short but manly appeal. When the civil war broke out Orlando did not indeed, as was the case with several lawyers, throw aside the gown for the sword; but he went into the north, and in the city of Chester, and elsewhere, did the King good service by affording the royal troops all the assistance in his power, in co-operation with his father, the Bishop of the diocese. Clarendon tells us how 'the city of Chester remained true to his Majesty, influenced thereto by the credit and example of Bishop John Bridgeman, and the reputation and dexterity of his son Orlando, a lawyer of very good estimation.' For these proofs of loyalty Bridgeman was expelled the House of Commons, and the Bishop's estates sequestrated. But when Charles summoned the members of both Houses that had been faithful to him, to his own Parliament at Oxford, Orlando Bridgeman took his seat as member for Wigan, in Christchurch Hall, and was there nominated by patent (sealed by Lord-Keeper Lyttleton) to the post of Attorney-General of the Court of Wards and Liveries, 'an office,' says Lord Campbell, 'when actually exercised, of great importance and emolument, but now a mere feather in his cap, which Parliament would not allow him to wear in their sight. At the time of the Treaty of Uxbridge, Bridgeman was chosen one of the Commissioners, and was thereto designated by his new title, but the potentates of Westminster would not acknowledge the appointment as valid, and treated him as plain Orlando Bridgeman.' When Oxford capitulated to Fairfax, he retired to his country house at Morton, where he was joined by the Bishop, and afterwards he proceeded privately to London.

During the interregnum he refused to put on his gown or to plead, but contented himself with acting as a conveyancer or chamber counsel. Yet we are informed that he took great note of passing events, whether judicial or political, and though he prudently abstained from any small plot hatching in the King's name, which he considered would be prejudicial to the royal cause, yet to the great measures which affected the Restoration our lawyer gave his strong adherence, and rejoiced in the return of Charles the Second to England. He had quick promotion, being made Serjeant-at-Law, Lord Chief Baron of the Exchequer, and Speaker of the House of Lords in the absence of the Lord Chancellor. His conduct on the trial of the regicides has naturally been differently judged, according to the bias of party feeling, but at all events his eloquence in charging the jury was highly extolled at the time, and when he had concluded the applause was so great that Judge Bridgeman felt himself called upon to check the expression thereof, saying, 'that it was more suitable for the audience of a stage-play rather than a court of justice.' His language indeed was rather fantastic and flowery, but that was the fashion at the time. He explained that 'the treason of the prisoners consisted not only in compassing and imagining the King's death, but in executing him in front of his own palace; in fact, not only laying the cockatrice's egg, but brooding upon the same, until it had brought forth a serpent!' On the expiration of the trials, Bridgeman was made a Baronet and Chief-Justice of the Common Pleas; and it was said of him that while presiding in this Court his reputation was at its zenith, and 'his moderation and equity were such that he seemed to carry a chancery in his breast.' In the intrigues which were being carried on against Lord Clarendon, Sir Orlando took no part; indeed his conduct was invariably marked by generosity towards the man whom he was destined to supplant, and he did all in his power to prevent the Chancellor's impeachment. In 1667 he was appointed Lord-Keeper at the instigation of some of the King's advisers, male and female, and it was whispered among his enemies that in that capacity he was at first more complaisant than his predecessor in affixing the great seal to royal grants, in favour of such personages as Lady Castlemaine, and others of her calibre. Be this as it may, the atrocious proceedings of the Cabal roused the Lord-Keeper into resistance, and the opposition he offered to these unscrupulous men hastened his downfall. His own family were also most prejudicial to his prosperity, his wife being an 'intriguer and intermeddler,' combining with his sons in matters with which they had no concern. Bridgeman was losing favour at Court; he had lately made himself obnoxious to the King and his surroundings by opposing many of their measures, and when he refused to confirm the Act of Toleration on the ground of illegality, Lord Shaftesbury hastened to Charles's presence bent on mischief, for that nobleman had long had his eyes greedily directed towards the Great Seal, and he became very eloquent in counting up all Sir Orlando's misdemeanours, ending by his *disinterested* advice for that minister's instant dismissal. Charles took a little time to be persuaded, but after a while he sent off secretary Coventry to demand the bone of contention from the Lord-Keeper. Bridgeman was all unprepared for the hasty and peremptory message, but he had no option, and the Great Seal was delivered to the royal messenger. Charles kept it in his own custody all night, and the next morning consigned it with the title of Lord Chancellor into the willing hands of Anthony Ashley Cooper. After his dismissal from office Sir Orlando retired to his villa near Teddington, where he died, and was buried. He was twice married—first to Judith, daughter and heir of John Kynaston, Esq. of Morton, County Salop, who died at Oxford, during the usurpation, and was there buried. He had an only son, Sir John Bridgeman, his successor. Sir Orlando had for his second wife, Dorothy, daughter of Dr. Saunders, Provost of Oriel College, Oxford, and relict of George Cradock, Esq. of Carsewell Castle, County Stafford, by whom he had two sons and one daughter, namely, Sir Orlando, created a Baronet; Sir Francis, knighted in 1673, who married Susanna, daughter and heir of Sir Richard Barker, Knight, but had no children; and Charlotte, married to Sir Thomas Myddleton of Chirk Castle.

As must invariably be the case with men in prominent positions, more especially in times of great civil, religious, and political struggles, Sir Orlando Bridgeman's character was by turns eulogised and blamed; in spite of his loyal services to Charles the First, that King found occasion to censure his faithful servant at the time of the Treaty of Uxbridge, on a question of religion, 'having,' said his Majesty, 'expected otherwise from the son of a Bishop.' Yet Sir Orlando was a staunch Churchman. Burnet's testimony was merely to his judicial capacity. He said: 'Bridgeman's practice was so entirely in common law that he did not seem to understand what equity was.' Roger North said: 'He was a celebrated lawyer, and sat with high esteem in the place of Chief-Justice of Common Pleas: the moving him then to the Chancery did not contribute to his fame'; while elsewhere we are told 'he carried a chancery in his breast.' 'He grew timorous, which was not mended by age; he laboured to please everybody, and that is a temper of ill consequence in a judge.' On the other hand, Lord Nottingham writes: 'It is due to the memory of so great a man to mention him with reverence and veneration for his learning and integrity.' While Lord Ellenborough extols him as an eminent judge, distinguished by the profundity of his learning and the extent of his industry. At all events, there is no doubt that the name of Sir Orlando Bridgeman, Lord-Keeper of the Great Seal, continues to be honoured, not only in the annals of his own family, but in the learned profession of the Law.

No. 5.
JOHN BRIDGEMAN, BISHOP OF CHESTER, FATHER OF THE LORD-KEEPER.

Black gown and ruff. Shield episcopal. Arms of Chester, impaling Bridgeman. Dated 1616. Aged 41.

BORN 1575, DIED 1657-8.

BY JANSEN.

EDWARD BRIDGEMAN was the younger son of William Bridgeman of Dean Parva, in the county of Gloucester. He settled in the city of Exeter, and was, in 1578, High-Sheriff of the said city and the county of Devon. His son John was born in Exeter, in a house not far from the palace-gate, which seemed an omen of his future dignity. He was a studious boy, and loved his books, and was carefully kept at school until it was deemed advisable 'to transplant him to the University,' when he was entered at Magdalen College, Cambridge, of which he became a Fellow, and eventually the Master. In 1600, being M.A., he was admitted *ad eundem* at Oxford, and here he attained the degree of Doctor of Divinity, being the highest, we are told, 'a scholar can receive, or the University bestow.' Dr. Bridgeman's character for learning and piety, combined with refinement of manners and good breeding, had reached the ears of King James the First, who appointed him one of his Domestic Chaplains, and soon afterwards he became incumbent of Wigan in Lancashire. For upwards of two hundred years, even to the present day, the living in question has been held, with scarcely any intermission, by a member of the family of Bridgeman. In 1619 the Doctor was raised to the See of Chester, being consecrated at Lambeth, at the same time as the Bishops of Oxford and Bristol. Now the King taking into consideration that the Bishopric of Chester was less lucrative than some others, His Majesty also preferred John Bridgeman to the living of Bangor in Wales, which he was to hold *ad commendam*, or temporarily. Collins tells us that his Lordship was not present in the Upper House, in the year 1641, when the bishops protested against the proceedings in Parliament, and were impeached, and sent to the Tower, whereby he was saved the tedious imprisonment to which his right reverend brethren were subjected. But all his proclivities were Royalist, and during the usurpation, his estates being sequestrated, he took refuge at his son's country house at Moreton, near Oswestry, in Salop, where he died about the year 1657 or 1658, being buried in the neighbouring church of Kinnerley, and not in the Cathedral of Chester, as some writers have it.

This worthy Prelate was said to have been 'as ingenious as he was brave, and a great patron of those gifts in others which he himself owned. He, moreover, was the father of that great and good man, Sir Orlando Bridgeman, the Lord-Keeper, who was a glory to his family, and indeed to the country at large.' The Bishop of Chester married Elizabeth, daughter of Dr. Helyar (of a good old Somersetshire family), Canon of Exeter, and Archdeacon of Barnstaple, by whom he had five sons—

1. Sir Orlando Bridgeman, afterwards First Baronet, and eventually Lord-Keeper.

2. Dove, Prebendary of Chester, married Miss Bennet of Cheshire (who survived him), by whom he had one son, Charles, Archdeacon of Richmond, in Yorkshire, who died unmarried 1678. The widow of Dove Bridgeman married, as her second husband, Dr. John Halkett, Bishop of Lichfield.

3. Henry Bridgeman, who was indeed rich in church preferment, being successively Rector of Bangor and Barrow, and Bishop of the Isle of Man. He married Catherine, daughter

of Robert Lever, of Lancashire, Gent., by whom he had one daughter, who married Sir Thomas Greenhalgh of Brundlesham, County Lancaster.

4. Sir James Bridgeman, Knight, who married the daughter of one Mr. Allen, a gentleman of Cheshire, by whom he had (beside a son and daughter, who died unmarried) Frances, wife of William, Lord Howard of Escrick, and Magdalen, wife of William Wynder, Esq.

5. Richard, a merchant in Amsterdam, married the daughter of one Mr. Watson, also an English merchant in that city, by whom he had a daughter, Elizabeth, married to John Dove, Surveyor of the Customs; and a son, William, of Westminster, some time Secretary of the Admiralty, and one of the Clerks of the Privy Council, who married Diana, daughter of Mr. Vernatti, an Italian gentleman. Their children were Orlando, and Catherine, married to a relative, son of Sir John Bridgeman, Bart.

No. 6.

SIR ORLANDO BRIDGEMAN, FOURTH BARONET.

Blue coat. Red overcoat. Wig.

DIED 1764.

BY VANDERBANK.

E was the son and successor of Sir John Bridgeman, third Baronet, by Ursula Matthews. He married Lady Anne Newport, daughter and co-heir of Richard, second Earl of Bradford, who, beside a large fortune, brought the beautiful estate of Weston into the Bridgeman family. Sir Orlando was for some time M.P. for Shrewsbury.

No. 7. HENRY NEWPORT, VISCOUNT NEWPORT, AFTERWARDS THIRD EARL OF BRADFORD.

Red coat. Silver brandebourgs.

DIED 1734.

BY DAHL.

E was the eldest son of Richard Newport, second Earl of Bradford, by Mary Wilbraham. He represented Shropshire in several Parliaments during his father's life, and was at different times Lord-Lieutenant and *Custos Rotulorum* of the Counties of Stafford, Shropshire, and Montgomery. Lord Bradford died unmarried at his house in St. James's Place, and was buried in Henry the Seventh's Chapel at Westminster.

He was succeeded in his titles, and such estates as he could not alienate, by his brother Thomas, who had become imbecile through a fall from his horse in early life in Cowhay Wood, Weston Park. He was incompetent to manage his own affairs, and, dying at Weston, 1762, his titles became extinct, and his property descended to his nephews, the sons of Lady Anne Bridgeman; and the Countess of Mountrath. Henry, Lord Bradford was an immoral and vindictive man, and having quarrelled with his mother on account of her endeavour to disentangle him from some disgraceful connection, he vowed vengeance on her and her whole family. This threat he carried out in a shameful manner, and though the story is long and complicated, yet it bears so nearly on the fortunes of the present possessor of Weston, that we cannot refrain from entering into details. In 1715, Lord Bradford cut off and debarred all the then existing entails of the family estates over which he had any power, and in 1730 he made a will by which he left all his large estates in trust, for the use of John Newport, *alias* Harrison, *alias* Smyth, his illegitimate son by Anne, wife of Ralph Smyth, son of the Dean of Raphoe, that lady being then Lord Bradford's mistress; the property to revert to the testator's lawful heirs in the event of the aforementioned John's death without children. But two days afterwards he repented of this partial act of compensation, and added a codicil by which he left the same property to the same trustees, in case of John's death without heirs, to his mother, Mrs. Anne Smyth, for her own personal use, to be devised as she saw fit, provided that during John's lifetime she should set aside a proper sum for his use and maintenance, after which she might make any use she chose of the residue. Four days afterwards another codicil assured the lady in question a further sum of £10,000.

Lord Bradford died in 1734, and Mrs. Anne Smyth in 1742, having two months before her death made a will leaving all the property bequeathed her by the said Earl to one Alexander Small, a surgeon (excepting as before what was set aside for the maintenance of John Newport), until John should have attained his majority, which was not to be until he was twenty-six years old. In the event of John Newport's death without children, then the reversion and inheritance of the said estates she devised to William Pulteney, afterwards Earl of Bath, his heirs and assigns for ever. It would be tedious to relate all the legal proceedings which arose out of this eccentric will; suffice it to say that it could not be proved till 1751, nine years after the death of the testatrix. Lord Bath on his part devised the reversion of the property expectant on the death of John Newport, to his brother, General Harry Pulteney, who in turn devised it to the daughter of his cousin-german (Daniel Pulteney), Frances, wife of William Johnstone, and her said husband (who afterwards became a baronet, and took the name of Pulteney), and to their heirs in tail male, with remainder to Harry, Earl of Darlington, whose grandmother was Anne Pulteney, aunt to the Earl of Bath, and daughter of Sir William Pulteney of Misterton, County Leicester and his sons in tail male.

All these aforementioned legatees died in succession without male heirs, excepting the Earl of Darlington, who left an only son, afterwards Duke of Cleveland, on whom the whole of this enormous fortune devolved, and is part of the heritage of the present Duke (1888). Thus the ancient estates of the Newports, including those which descended to them from the Princes of South Wales, passed away from the rightful owners, excepting Weston-under-Lizard, Walsall, and some other estates elsewhere mentioned, which became the property of Sir Henry Bridgeman, grandson of Mary, Countess of Bradford. The savings from the estate during the lifetime of John Newport, which were said to exceed £200,000, were ultimately divided (after deducting the great law charges) between the Crown (to which it passed in default of heirs), and, through a ridiculous quibble of the law, the representatives of Ralph Smyth (John Newport's mother's husband).

No. 8. LADY ANNE BRIDGEMAN.

White satin dress. Leaning her arm on a table. Fair hair.

BORN 1690, DIED 1752.

BY VANDERBANK.

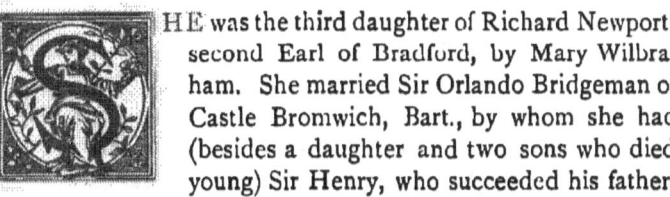

HE was the third daughter of Richard Newport, second Earl of Bradford, by Mary Wilbraham. She married Sir Orlando Bridgeman of Castle Bromwich, Bart., by whom she had (besides a daughter and two sons who died young) Sir Henry, who succeeded his father, and Diana, married to John Sawbridge of Ollantigh, in Kent.

This lady's descendants are now the only representatives of the ancient family of Newport.

No. 9.

HENRY, FOURTH LORD HERBERT OF RIPSFORD.

DIED 1691.

BY WISSING.

EDWARD, first Lord Herbert of Ripsford, the 'noble author' of whom Horace Walpole speaks in terms of the highest enthusiasm, and whose autobiography he published, was succeeded by his son Richard, who married a daughter of John, Earl of Bridgewater, by whom he had two surviving sons (who in turn succeeded to the title) and two daughters. The youngest, Florence, married her kinsman, Richard Herbert of Oakley Park. Edward, third Lord Herbert of Cherbury, a zealous loyalist, dying without children by either of his three wives, the titles and estates devolved on his brother Henry, who married Lady Catherine Newport, daughter of Francis, first Earl of Bradford. On the fourth Lord's decease *s.p.*, the title became extinct, but the dignity of Herbert of Cherbury was revived in favour of his nephew (son of his sister Florence), Henry Arthur Herbert, afterwards Earl of Powis, in 1743.

Catherine Newport, Lady Herbert, survived her husband, and resided till her death at Lymore in Montgomeryshire, the considerable estate belonging to Herbert which had been appointed her as her jointure. She was remarkable for her extensive charities.

No. 10. SIR JOHN BRIDGEMAN, SECOND BART.

Red dress. Holding a jewelled sword.

BORN 1630, DIED 1710.

BY VICTOR.

E was the eldest son of Sir Orlando Bridgeman, Lord Keeper, and the only child by that gentleman's 'first venter' (so runs a line in the learned gentleman's biography), Judith, daughter and heir of John Kynaston of Morton, in Shropshire, Esq. He married Mary, daughter and heir of George Cradock of Carsewell Castle, in Staffordshire, whose widow married Sir Orlando as his second wife. By this alliance John Bridgeman's mother-in-law became his step-mother, a singular relationship. He had four sons, three of whom died unmarried; the two who survived him were John, his namesake and successor, and Orlando, married to Catherine, daughter of William Bridgeman of Comb, County Suffolk, Esq. The daughters were Mary, married to Robert Lloyd, Esq. of Aston, in Shropshire; Judith, married to Richard Corbet of Morton Corbet, County Shropshire; Dorothy, wife of Lisle Hackett of Moxhull, County Warwick; and three others who died unmarried. Sir John died at his own house of Castle Bromwich, but was buried at Aston, in Warwickshire.

Principal Staircase.

No. 11.

FRANCIS NEWPORT, SECOND LORD NEWPORT, AND FIRST EARL OF BRADFORD.

Blue mantle. Long wig.

BORN 1619, DIED 1708.

BY DAHL.

E was the eldest son of Sir Richard Newport, Kt. of High Ercall, who was knighted by King James the First, at Theobalds, and, in 1642, in consequence of his unswerving loyalty to King Charles the First, created Baron Newport. Sir Richard married Rachel, daughter of Sir John Leveson, Kt. of Haling, or Halington, County Kent, and sister to Sir Richard Leveson of Trentham, County Stafford, Knight of the Bath. Francis was the first born of a large family, and began public life at an early age, being chosen to represent the borough of Shrewsbury in Parliament, a few days after he had attained his majority. He was one of the few members (fifty-six in number) who had the courage to vote for the acquittal of Lord Strafford, a proceeding which brought down on the heads of the so-called 'Straffordians' both insult and obloquy. He followed in the footsteps of his father, declared for the Royal cause in the unhappy differences between Charles and his Parliament, and was soon expelled the House of Commons as a 'malignant.' He took arms in the Royal army, and did gallant service in the field, till he was made prisoner at Oswestry, when that town was taken by the Earl of Denbigh and Colonel Mytton. At the time of the insurrection in North Wales, Francis Newport proved himself a zealous friend to Charles the Second, and as powerful as he was zealous. He was also engaged in the unsuccessful siege of Shrewsbury, which town, in the beginning of the ensuing year, was once more in the hands of the Royalists. On this occasion, as we have mentioned elsewhere, Sir Edward Hyde (Lord Clarendon) was sorely puzzled as to the respective claims to the Governorship of Shrewsbury, between Sir Thomas Myddleton, and his friend, Francis Newport. Two months after the restoration of the King (May 29, 1660), Lord Newport was appointed Lord-Lieutenant and *Custos Rotulorum* of Shropshire, and later on, by Charles the Second, Comptroller and Treasurer of the Household, and a Privy Councillor. In 1674 he was advanced to the title of Viscount Newport of Bradford, County Salop, and, on the accession of James the Second, his lordship was continued in all his former offices for a time, but he was a true patriot, and the arbitrary and unconstitutional measures of the new King called forth in him a vigorous opposition. So open was he in the expression of his political opinions that he was not only superseded in all his offices at Court, but was also removed from the Lord-Lieutenancy of Shropshire, which was given up to the unworthy hands of the Lord Chancellor Jefferies. He upheld the cause of religion at the trial of the seven Bishops, and, being a firm Protestant, he voted for the succession of the Prince and Princess of Orange. On the day that William and Mary were proclaimed, Lord Newport was reinstated in his posts in the Royal Household and his Lord-Lieutenancy of Shropshire, in all of which offices he continued until he attained the age of eighty-four, when they devolved on his son. In 1694 he was created Earl of Bradford, and on the accession of Queen Anne again sworn of the Privy Council. Lord Newport was an object of special dislike to James the Second, as we find from one of the ex-King's declarations (respecting a projected descent upon England), that this nobleman would certainly be debarred from all hope of pardon. Lord Bradford died at Twickenham in his eighty-ninth year, and was buried at Wroxeter, near his country house of Eyton, in Shropshire, where a marble monument on the south wall of the chancel bears a long inscription to his memory. It was written of him that 'at the time of his death, he was the most venerable character of any nobleman in England, on account of his virtues, and the unblemished honour with which he had filled every station of life. Equally a friend to the clergy and to the poor, having enlarged the endowments of several poor vicarages, and erected a charitable foundation at Ercall for the support of the needy.' King William had so great a regard for the Earl of Bradford, that he paid him a visit, and honoured him with his presence at dinner on his eightieth birthday. He married Lady Diana Russell, daughter of the fourth Earl of Bedford, by whom he had a large family, five dying in their infancy; and

Richard, second Earl of Bradford;

Francis, who died unmarried;

Thomas, a Commissioner of the Customs in the reigns of William and Mary, and Queen Anne, who, in the first year of George the First was made a Lord of the Treasury and raised to the peerage by the title of Baron Torrington of Torrington, County Devon, and sworn of the Privy Council. He was also at the time of his death a Teller of the Exchequer. He had three wives: first, Lucy, daughter of Sir Edward Atkyns, Lord Chief Justice of the Exchequer in the time of James the Second; second, Penelope, daughter of Sir Orlando Bridgeman of Ridley, County Chester, Bart., who died in 1705; third, Anne, daughter of Robert Pierrepoint of Nottingham, Esq., son of Francis Pierrepoint, and grandson of Robert, Earl of Kingston. He died the 27th of May 1719, in the sixty-fifth year of his age (when his title became extinct), and lies buried at Wroxeter with Anne, his third wife, who survived him many years, and died on the 7th February 1734.

No. 12.   LADY WILBRAHAM.

Pale yellow dress.   Grey drapery.   Pointing to a tulip.

By Sir Peter Lely.

LIZABETH, daughter and sole heir of Edward Mytton, Esq. of Weston-under-Lizard, which place he inherited through females from the ancient possessors. She married Sir Thomas Wilbraham of Woodhey, Bart., by whom she had three daughters, co-heiresses, who each inherited a large property, both landed and funded, from both parents. They were, Charlotte, wife of Sir Thomas Myddleton of Chirk Castle; Mary, Countess of Bradford; and Grace, Countess of Dysart.

No. 13.

SIR THOMAS WILBRAHAM, BART.

Red coat.   Blue mantle.

By Verelst.

HE family of Wilbraham, or, as it was formerly written, Wilburgham, derived its name from a manor in Cambridgeshire, where it was settled in the reign of Henry the Second. They afterwards removed to Cheshire, where they became much respected and very influential. The subject of the present notice was the son of Sir Thomas Wilbraham, of Woodhey, County Chester, by the daughter of Sir Roger Wilbraham of Bridgemoor, in the

same county. He married the daughter and sole heir of Edward Mytton, Esq., of Weston-under-Lizard, by whom he had three daughters, co-heiresses. The direct male line of a very ancient Cheshire family ended in the person of Sir Thomas Wilbraham.

No. 14.

SIR JOHN BRIDGEMAN, THIRD BARONET.

As a youth. Blue and gold dress.

DIED 1747.

BY VICTOR.

E was the son of Sir John Bridgeman, second baronet (the only son of the Lord Keeper by his 'first venter,' so runs an old biography), by the daughter and co-heir of George Cradock of Carsewell, County Stafford. He was the eldest surviving of many children, and married Ursula, daughter and sole heir of Roger Matthews of Blodwell, County Salop; by whom he had a large family, both sons and daughters, of whom only two survived, namely, Orlando, his successor, and a daughter, married to Hugh Williams, Esq.

No. 15. FAMILY GROUP.

HENRY BRIDGEMAN, *first Lord Bradford; yellow dress, hat and feathers.* LADY BRADFORD, *in green. The eldest daughter in a pink gown, playing the harpsichord. Her sister in a white gown, playing the harp.* ORLANDO *in red.* JOHN *in blue.* GEORGE *sitting on the step near the pianoforte.*

BY PINE.

SIR HENRY BRIDGEMAN, BART., FIRST BARON BRADFORD.

BORN 1725, DIED 1800.

HE eldest surviving son of Sir Orlando Bridgeman, by Lady Anne Newport, daughter of the second Earl of Bradford. He sat in Parliament for many years, and in 1794 was advanced to the Peerage, as Baron Bradford of Bradford, County Salop. He married Elizabeth, daughter and heir of John Simpson, Esq., by whom he had a large family. His wife, three sons, and two daughters are represented in this group, namely, Orlando, his successor, John (Bridgeman Simpson), George, Rector of Wigan. The daughters married Henry Greswolde Lewis of Malvern Hall, Esq., and Sir George William Gunning, Bart.

No. 16.

THE HONOURABLE MRS. GUNNING.

White lace cap, and fichu.

BORN 1764, DIED 1810.

BY HOPPNER.

SHE was the younger daughter of Henry Bridgeman, first Lord Bradford, by Miss Simpson; married in 1794 George William, only son of Sir Robert Gunning of Horton, County North Hants, by whom she had several children.

No. 17.

ELIZABETH, WIFE OF JOHN BRIDGEMAN, BISHOP OF CHESTER.

Black dress. Cap.

DIED 1636.

AFTER JANSEN.

SHE was the daughter of Dr. Helyar, Canon of Exeter and Archdeacon of Barnstaple, of an ancient family in Somersetshire. She married John Bridgeman, Bishop of Chester, famed alike for his piety and his loyalty, by whom she was the mother of five sons:—1. Sir Orlando, afterwards Lord Keeper; 2. Dove, Prebendary of the Cathedral Church of Chester; 3. Henry, Dean of Chester;

4. Sir James, Knight; 5. Richard, a merchant in Amsterdam, whose grand-daughter married her kinsman, Orlando Bridgeman, fourth son of the second Baronet, and grandson of the Lord Keeper.

Mrs. Bridgeman was buried in Chester Cathedral.

No. 19. ORLANDO BRIDGEMAN, ESQUIRE.

Black coat. Blue overcoat on left arm. Long black wig.

BORN 1671, DIED 1721.

BY DAHL.

E was the fifth son of Sir John Bridgeman, second Baronet, by Mary, daughter of George Cradock, Esquire, of Carsewell Castle, County Stafford. Orlando was M.P. for Wigan, and married his cousin Katherine, daughter of William Bridgeman, Esquire of Coombes, Secretary to the Admiralty.

No. 20.

CHARLOTTE BRIDGEMAN.

As a child. In a white frock. With an Italian greyhound.

BORN 1761, DIED 1802.

DAUGHTER of Henry, first Lord Bradford, afterwards the Honourable Mrs. Greswolde Lewis.

No. 21. VISCOUNTESS TORRINGTON.

Brown gown. Black mob cap.

BORN 1744, DIED 1792.

BY GAINSBOROUGH.

HE was the daughter of John Boyle, Earl of Cork and Orrery, by his second wife, Margaret Hamilton of Caledon, County Tyrone. She married, in 1765, George, fourth Viscount Torrington, by whom she had four daughters—Lady John Russell, the Countess of Bradford, the Marchioness of Bath, and Emily, married to Henry, eldest son of Lord Robert Seymour.

No. 22.

LIONEL TOLLEMACHE, SECOND EARL OF DYSART.

Brown dress. Wig.

BORN 1648, DIED 1727.

BY RILEY.

E was the son of Sir Lionel Tollemache of Helmingham, County Norfolk, by Lady Elizabeth Murray, elder daughter and heir of William Murray, Lord Huntingtower, first Earl of Dysart. These honours were conferred on William Murray, a member of a younger branch of the house of Tullibardine by Charles the First, with remainder to heirs male and female. His eldest

daughter, Elizabeth, married Sir Lionel Tollemache, and succeeded her father as Countess of Dysart in her own right, having obtained from Charles the Second, in 1670, a confirmation of her honours, with a clause in the charter allowing her to nominate any one of her children she pleased as her heir. After the death of Sir Lionel Tollemache, his widow married the Duke of Lauderdale, and dying in 1697 was succeeded by her eldest son, Sir Lionel Tollemache, as Lord Huntingtower and Earl of Dysart. He was M.P. for Orford in 1678 and 1685, and represented the County of Suffolk until he was incapacitated from sitting in the House by the passing of the Act of Union with Scotland. He had declined an English barony upon the accession of Queen Anne. He married, in 1680, Grace, daughter and co-heir of Sir Thomas Wilbraham, by whom he had a son and two daughters. The eldest son, who married Miss Cavendish, died *v.p.*, and their son succeeded his grandfather as Earl of Dysart.

No. 23.

PORTRAIT OF A YOUNG LADY.   UNKNOWN.

BY MRS. BEALE.

CIRCULAR STAIRCASE.

CIRCULAR STAIRCASE.

No. I.

HENRY RICH, EARL OF HOLLAND.

Cuirass. White sleeves embroidered in gold. Lace collar. Belt over right, Ribbon over left shoulder.

EXECUTED 1649.

BY H. STONE.

THE second son of Robert Rich, first Earl of Warwick, by Lady Penelope Devereux, daughter of Walter, Earl of Essex. He went to France and Holland in his youth, and returning to England appeared at Court, where he attracted the notice and favour of George, Duke of Buckingham, who was then all-powerful with King James the First. It appears to have been through Buckingham's intervention that he married the rich heiress of Sir John Cope of Kensington, of which place Rich shortly bore the title of Baron. He also held offices at Court about the King's person, and that of Henry Prince of Wales; was made Earl of Holland, Knight of the Garter, Privy Councillor, and sent Ambassador to negotiate the marriage of Prince Charles, first in Spain and afterwards in France. On the latter occasion it was rumoured that his beauty and courtliness made a deep impression on the heart of his future Queen, Henrietta Maria.

Clarendon says of him that 'he was of a lovely and winning presence, and genteel conversation.' He also accompanied the Duke of Buckingham to Holland on a diplomatic mission. On the first breaking out of an insurrection of the Scots, he was made General of the Horse, and though not in arms at the commencement of the Civil War, when evil days fell on the King, Lord Holland joined him with many other loyal noblemen, and on his being appointed General of the Royal army, numbers flocked to ask commissions from him. In 1648, after many fluctuations of fortune, he was pursued and taken prisoner near St. Neot's in Huntingdonshire, whence he was conveyed to Warwick House, and finally to the Tower, and a High Court of Justice was appointed to sit for the trial of the Earl of Holland, the Duke of Hamilton, and other Peers. He was in ill-health at the time, and when examined answered little, 'as a man who would rather receive his life from their favour than from the strength of his defence.' He was condemned, however, in spite of the influence of his brother, the Earl of Warwick, and the exertions of the Presbyterian party. There was not a large majority against him, but Cromwell, it would appear, disliked him extremely, and accordingly on the 9th of March 1649, Lord Holland suffered death immediately after the Duke of Hamilton.

Spent by long sickness, he addressed but few words to the people, recommending them with his last breath to uphold the King's government and the established religion.

He left four sons and five daughters. Robert, the eldest, succeeded to his father's honours, and likewise to the Earldom of Warwick on the death of his uncle in 1672.

No. 2.

FRANCIS NEWPORT, FIRST EARL OF BRADFORD.

Blue dress. Long wig.

DIED 1708, AGED 88.

AFTER DAHL.

No. 3.

HENRI DE LA TOUR D'AUVERGNE, MARSHAL TURENNE.

Brown dress. Armour.

BORN 1611, KILLED IN ACTION 1675.

THE second son of the Duke de Bouillon, by Elizabeth of Nassau, daughter of William the Silent and Charlotte de Montpensier. His father being one of the chief Calvinist leaders, brought up his two sons, the Prince de Sedan and the Vicomte de Turenne, in the most rigid tenets of that party. From early childhood young Turenne had set his heart on becoming a soldier, and many interesting anecdotes are recorded of his boyish enthusiasm. His military exploits, his daring gallantry and skill as a commander, have made his name world-renowned, and the battles that he won, the wonderful vicissitudes of his career, both political and military, belong to the pages of European history.

He was killed by a stray shot at the beginning of an engagement with the Imperialist troops near the village of Salzbach. His death was deeply deplored by his soldiery, of whom he was the idol, and caused general consternation in Paris. Madame de Sévigné in one of her letters gives a most graphic account of the effect produced by the news of his death at Court, which, for a time, suspended the usual routine of festivity.

EAST STAIRCASE.

EAST STAIRCASE.

No. 2.　　　　LORD LYNEDOCH.
Black coat. Fur collar. White waistcoat. Cutlass under left arm.
DIED 1843.
BY SIR GEORGE HAYTER.

THOMAS GRAHAM of Balgowan, created Baron Lynedoch in 1814, having distinguished himself by his services in the Peninsular War, more especially at the victory of Barossa, in 1811. He married, in 1774, the Honourable Mary Cathcart, daughter of Charles, ninth Lord Cathcart, who died in 1792. They had no children, and on the death of Lord Lynedoch, the title became extinct, and the estate of Balgowan devolved upon his kinsman, Robert Graham, Esq.

No. 5.
PORTRAIT OF A LADY. UNKNOWN.
Pale grey and green dress. Holding a nosegay. Red curtains.

No. 6.

GEORGE A. F. H. BRIDGEMAN, VISCOUNT
NEWPORT, AFTERWARDS SECOND
EARL OF BRADFORD.

Brown coat. Fur collar. White neckcloth.

BORN 1789, DIED 1865.

BY SIR GEORGE HAYTER.

HE was the son of the first Earl of Bradford of the Bridgeman family, by the Hon. Lucy Byng. He married as his first wife, in 1818, Georgina, only daughter of Sir Thomas Moncreiffe, Bart., of Moncreiffe, by whom he had Orlando George, his successor, the present Earl; the Hon. and Rev. George Bridgeman, rector of Wigan; the Hon. and Rev. John Bridgeman, rector of Weston; and four daughters. Lady Bradford died in 1842, and the Earl married, secondly, Helen, widow of Sir David Moncreiffe, Bart., and daughter of Æneas Mackay, Esq. of Scotston, Peebles. She died in 1869.

Without taking an active part in politics, his principles were those of a staunch Conservative. He was an excellent landlord, and took delight in enlarging and improving his property. In his family he was beloved; in his household highly respected. He wrote a book entitled *Letters from Portugal, Spain, and Sicily*, when he travelled to those countries, accompanied by Lord John Russell and the Hon. Robert Clive, in 1812. This volume was privately printed in 1875 by his son, the present Earl, and showed him to have been a man of culture and refinement of taste, more especially in points of art and literature. In both branches he distinguished himself as a collector. The Vicar of Tong, who had known Lord Bradford intimately for upwards of twenty years, in a speech made at a public dinner, speaks in the highest terms of his deceased patron, of his unaffected piety and of his profound sense of justice, and holds him up as an example to the surviving generation.

No. 7.   MARQUESS OF DALHOUSIE.

Black coat. Ribbon. Order of the Thistle, and Star.

BORN 1812, DIED 1860.

BY CLARK AFTER SIR J. WATSON GORDON.

JAMES ANDREW RAMSAY was the third but eldest surviving son of George, ninth Earl of Dalhousie, by Christian, daughter of Charles Broun, Esq. of Colstoun, Haddingtonshire. He married, in 1836, Lady Susan Georgiana, daughter of George, Marquess of Tweeddale, and by her (who died on her voyage home from India in 1853) had two daughters. Lord Dalhousie was appointed Governor-General of India in 1847, and retained that office till 1856. He was created Marquess of Dalhousie of Dalhousie Castle, and of the Punjab, for his eminent services in 1849.

On his death in 1860, the Marquessate became extinct, and he was succeeded in the Earldom by his cousin.

No. 8.

ORLANDO GEORGE CHARLES BRIDGEMAN, THIRD AND PRESENT EARL OF BRADFORD.

Full-length. Black velvet coat. Blue tie. Boots and spurs. Riding-whip. Black retriever at his feet. Background landscape.

BORN 1819.

BY SIR FRANCIS GRANT.

No. 13.

THE DUKE OF WELLINGTON.

Oval. Dark cloak. White neckcloth.

BORN 1769, DIED 1852.

BY SIR GEORGE HAYTER.

THE Iron Duke, the hero of the Peninsular War and Waterloo, warrior, patriot, statesman. His biography belongs to the annals of his country.

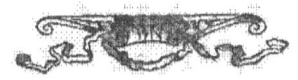

BEDROOMS.

BEDROOM A.

No. 3.   MARY QUEEN OF SCOTS.

Red dress, embroidered.   Pearls and cross.   Jewels in her hair.
AFTER ZUCCHERO.

No. 6.   MARY YATES.

An old woman in a white cap looking out of an oval stone window. She holds a board on which is inscribed ' Mary Yates, aged 127 years. Born at Wheaton Aston, in Staffordshire. She enjoyed her senses till her death, but she was helpless five years before she died, which was in August 1776.   G.B.I.'   '*Colombo pinxit.*'

No. 7.

ELIZABETH, LADY BRADFORD.

In crayons.   Seated in a landscape.   Red habit.   Blue waistcoat. With a little dog beside her.
DIED 1806.

SHE was the daughter and heir of the Rev. John Simpson, and married in 1755 Sir Henry Bridgeman, afterwards created in 1794 Baron Bradford.

No. 8. HENRY, LORD BRADFORD.

Blue coat. White vest. Powder. Black retriever. In crayons.

DIED 1800.

HE was the only son of Sir Orlando Bridgeman by Lady Ann Newport. In Sir Henry's person the title of Bradford was revived, he being, in 1794, created Baron Bradford. He married Elizabeth Simpson, who survived him, and had by her four sons.

No. 10.

LUCY BYNG, DOWAGER COUNTESS OF BRADFORD.

Crayons. A head. She wears a bonnet, with her hair in curls.

DIED 1844.

BY SIR WILLIAM ROSS.

SHE was the daughter of George Byng, fourth Viscount Torrington, by Lady Lucy Boyle. She married, in 1788, Orlando Bridgeman, afterwards first Earl of Bradford, who died in 1825.

No. 11. HAMET BEN HAMET.

In Oriental costume.

BY SIR GODFREY KNELLER.

Bedroom A.

No. 13.

HON. MRS. BRIDGEMAN SIMPSON.

High white dress and blue sash. Powder. Large hat.

DIED 1791.

HE was the only daughter of Sir Thomas Worsley of Appuldercombe, Isle of Wight, and married, in 1784, the Hon. John Bridgeman (son of Henry, the first Baron Bradford), who had assumed the surname of Simpson in right of his mother, and had three children —a son and daughter who died young, and Henrietta, heiress of her uncle, Sir Richard Worsley. Henrietta married Lord Yarborough.

No. 14.

SIR THOMAS MONCREIFFE, SEVENTH BARONET, AND HIS SISTER.

Two children seated. The girl's arm round her brother's neck. Background, landscape. White dress. Blue sash. Holding flowers.

BORN 1822, DIED 1879.

BY SIR WILLIAM ROSS.

E was the son of Sir David Moncreiffe, sixth Baronet, by Helen, daughter of Æneas Mackay, Esq. of Scotston, and succeeded to his father as seventh baronet in 1830. Sir Thomas married, in 1843, Lady Louisa Hay, daughter of the tenth Earl of Kinnoull, by whom he had a very large family.

His sister Helen married, in 1844, Edmund Wright, Esq. of Halston, Shropshire, and died in 1874.

BEDROOM B.

No. 1.   THE QUEEN (WHOM GOD PRESERVE !).

Half-length.   Black dress.   White cap.

BY J. BLAKE WIRGMAN.

PAINTED at Osborne by Her Majesty's special permission for the Earl of Bradford.

No. 3.

CAPTAIN THOMAS MORTIMER, ADJUTANT,
SHROPSHIRE MILITIA.

Red uniform.   Gold epaulettes.   Grey hair.

BY J. WEAVER, 1819.

No. 4.   THE DUKE OF WELLINGTON.

Black coat.   White waistcoat.   Order of the Golden Fleece.   Ribbon of the Garter.   The town in the background.   Three-quarters length.

BY SIR GEORGE HAYTER.

No. 7.   COUNTESS OF KINGSTON.

Blue dress. Little dog at her feet.

BY MRS. BEALE.

SHE was the wife of William Pierrepont, fourth Earl of Kingston, and daughter of Robert, Lord Brooke.

No. 11.   LORD JOHN RUSSELL.

Black dress. Holding a roll.

BORN 1792, DIED 1878.

BY SIR GEORGE HAYTER.

E was the youngest son of Lord John Russell, afterwards sixth Duke of Bedford, by the Honourable Georgiana Elizabeth Byng. In an able article in the *Times* of 1878 mention is thus made of this eminent statesman :—

' He took an early interest in politics, and by the time he left college his political faith had crystalised into something very like that in which he lived, laboured, and died.' A visit to the Peninsula, where the star of Wellington was then in the ascendant, modified his French ideas (he had commenced by being an ardent advocate of the Revolution in France) and inspired young Russell with such an admiration for the hero that ever afterwards in the fiercest political struggle he maintained towards the Duke the attitude and language of profound admiration. His subsequent career belongs to the history of his country. He was a zealous upholder of Catholic Emancipation, and in the cause of Parliamentary Reform was the leading spirit, the draft for the first Bill of which was drawn up by his own hand. He sat for numerous constituencies in the House of Commons for a period of forty-seven years, during many of which he was the leader of the Opposition. He filled many of the highest offices of State, and was First Lord of the Treasury from 1846 to 1852. In 1865 he was again at the head of the Government from which he retired in 1866, having been raised to the peerage as Earl Russell and Viscount Amberley in 1861, and created a K.G.

His first wife was Adelaide, daughter of Thomas Lister of Armitage Park, widow of the second Lord Ribblesdale (who died in 1838 leaving two daughters).

His second wife was Lady Frances Elliot, daughter of Gilbert, second Earl of Minto, by whom he had three sons and a daughter.

Lord Russell was an author as well as a statesman, and published several works political, historical, dramatic, etc. He died at Pembroke Lodge in Richmond Park.

No. 12.

THE HONOURABLE HENRY BRIDGEMAN.

Crayons. Black gown.

BORN 1795, DIED 1872.

BY SHARPLES.

THE son of the first Earl of Bradford. He married in 1820 his first cousin Louisa, daughter of the Honourable John Bridgeman Simpson. Was a clergyman of the Church of England, but afterwards embraced the Irvingite doctrine.

Bedroom B.

No. 15.

THE REV. LEONARD CHAPPELOW.

In pastel. An old gentleman seated on a rock with a stick and book. Wears his hat.

BY SHARPLES.

HE was chaplain to Henry, Lord Bradford.

No. 16.

ORLANDO BRIDGEMAN, ESQ., SON OF SIR HENRY, WHO WAS AFTERWARDS CREATED LORD BRADFORD.

In pastel. Blue coat. Buff waistcoat.

No. 17.

ORLANDO BRIDGEMAN, FIRST EARL OF BRADFORD.

Seated. Black coat. White waistcoat. Right hand in his bosom.

PAINTED IN 1822.

BEDROOM C.

No. 8.

MARIE ANNE CHRISTINE, PRINCESS OF BAVARIA.

Low grey dress, cut square, trimmed with lace. Black headdress and white feather. Necklace and earrings.

BORN 1660, DIED 1690.

BY DE TROYES.

AUGHTER of Ferdinand, Elector of Bavaria. Born at Munich. Negotiations being set on foot for the marriage of this Princess with the Dauphin of France, King Louis the Fourteenth sent De Troyes to paint a portrait of her, and likewise a confidential envoy to give some description of his future daughter-in-law. The report was satisfactory; for although not a real beauty, Maria Christina possessed great perfection of form, and was lively and agreeable. She was united to Louis, Dauphin of France, in 1680, at Châlons-sur-Marne, where the French court repaired to do honour to the nuptials. Anxious to find favour in the eyes of her father-in-law, she perfectly succeeded in the attempt, for the King found her very accomplished, well-informed, of great conversational powers, and wonderfully ready at repartee, while her easy, unconstrained, though

refined manners surprised the court of the Louvre. The only drawback to the bride's popularity was her love of quiet and retirement; and after the festivities attending the celebration of the marriage were concluded, the Dauphine evinced her predilection for a small and intimate coterie, and the propensity to yield too implicitly to the influence of one of her Bavarian ladies, which caused some jealousy. Her time was fully occupied by reading and devotional exercises. The King strove in vain to wean her from pursuits which tended to seclusion from the world; but, finding his attempts useless, he no longer thwarted her inclinations. The Dauphine was very ill at the time of the birth of her third son, the Duc de Berry, and never recovered her health. When she felt her end approaching, she sent for the child, whom she embraced tenderly and blessed, concluding with these touching words: 'C'est de bon cœur quoique tu me coutes bien cher.' She also took a tender leave of her eldest son, the Duc de Bourgogne (father of Louis xv.). Louis the Fourteenth sat by the deathbed of his daughter-in-law, and when advised to withdraw, he said, 'No; it is better I should see how my equals die;' and he spoke some admonitory words in the same strain to the Dauphin, who was also present, on the transitory nature of earthly grandeur. The Dauphine's funeral oration was preached by Fléchier, and considered a *chef-d'œuvre.*

BEDROOM D.

Nos. 1 and 2.

PORTRAITS OF ORLANDO G. C., VISCOUNT NEWPORT (PRESENT AND THIRD EARL OF BRADFORD), AND SELINA, HIS WIFE.

Crayons. Modern dress. Turquoise necklace. Diamonds in her hair.

BOTH BY JAMES SWINTON, ESQ.

BEDROOM E.

No. 3.   THE QUEEN (WHOM GOD PRESERVE!).

*In an evening dress, pale blue and red.   Tiara, necklace, and earrings.
Red ribbon.   Gold jewelled chain.*

BY CLARKE AFTER WINTERHALTER.

MINIATURES.

MINIATURES.

[ONLY those that can be identified are named here, as there are several on the lids of snuff-boxes and elsewhere of which we cannot trace the originals.]

Five Miniatures in one frame which were given to the Earl of Bradford by Mr. Shirley in 1868.

1.

MISS WORSLEY, HEIRESS OF APPULDERCOMBE.

In powder.

She was the first wife of the Honourable John Bridgeman Simpson.

2.

THE HONOURABLE LUCY BYNG.

Reading.

She was wife of the first Earl of Bradford.

3.
THE HONOURABLE LUCY BYNG.
With a lace veil on her head.

4.
JOSEPHINE, EMPRESS OF THE FRENCH.
In a medallion.

5.
ELIZABETH, LADY BRADFORD.
White dress. Pearl necklace. Powder. On a snuff-box.

She was the wife of Henry Bridgeman, first Lord Bradford.

6.
THE HON. ELIZABETH BRIDGEMAN,
AFTERWARDS MRS. GUNNING.

Left by Sir George Gunning to the Countess of Bradford.

7.
MRS. SALKEN.

8.
ALEXANDER II., CZAR OF RUSSIA.
BORN 1818, MURDERED 1881.

On the lid of a snuff-box.

Presented by the Emperor to the third Earl of Bradford, when Master of the Horse in May 1874.

9.
LADY JOHN RUSSELL, Second Daughter of Viscount Torrington.

10.
THE SAME.
Her hair powdered.

11.
HON. LUCY BYNG, COUNTESS OF BRADFORD.

On a brooch which belonged to her sister, Mrs. Seymour, and was given to the Earl of Bradford by Lady Charles Russell, *née* Seymour.

12.
HON. O. G. C. BRIDGEMAN when two years old. Present and Third Earl of Bradford.

By Viscountess Newport after Anthony Stewart.

13.
HON. GEORGE BYNG.
Small oval.
DIED AN INFANT.

The son of the fourth Viscount Torrington by Lady Lucy Boyle.

14.
THE HON. ORLANDO AND MRS. BRIDGEMAN, afterwards First Earl and Countess of Bradford.
On a snuff-box.

15.
JOHN BOYLE, FIFTH EARL OF CORK AND ORRERY.

16.
MR. CHAPPELOW, AFTERWARDS CHAPLAIN TO THE EARL OF BRADFORD.
AGED 18.
Trencher-cap and college gown.

17.
WILLIAM THE FIRST, EMPEROR OF GERMANY.
On a snuff-box.
Presented by the Crown Prince to the third Earl of Bradford, when Master of the Horse in 1879.

18.
THE HON. ORLANDO BRIDGEMAN, AFTERWARDS FIRST EARL OF BRADFORD.

19.
A LADY MARKED AS 'MOTHER OF MARY SCOTT.'
Presented to the Earl of Bradford in 1844 by Mrs. Scott.

20.
LADY LUCY BRIDGEMAN, DAUGHTER OF EDMUND BOYLE, EARL OF CORK AND ORRERY.
Black silhouette.

21.
HON. AND REV. GEORGE BRIDGEMAN, Son of the First Lord Bradford, and Husband of the preceding.

22.
GEORGE BYNG, Fourth Viscount Torrington.
A circular miniature.

23.
LADY LUCY WHITMORE, Daughter of Orlando First Earl of Bradford, by the Hon. Lucy Byng.
Married W. Whitmore, Esq. of Dudmaston, Co. Salop.

24.
GENERAL VANDERNERCK.

25.
HON. MRS. BRIDGEMAN AND LADY JOHN RUSSELL.
In one case.

The Honourable Lucy and the Honourable Georgiana Byng—daughters of Lord Torrington—the former afterwards Countess of Bradford, to whom the miniatures were bequeathed by the Duke of Bedford.

26.
GEORGINA ELIZABETH, Wife of the Second Earl of Bradford (*née* Moncreiffe).
Painted by Sir W. Ross.

27.

THE TWO ELDEST CHILDREN OF THE SECOND EARL AND COUNTESS OF BRADFORD.

BY MISS MAGDALEN ROSS, 1828.

28.

GEORGE IV., KING OF ENGLAND.

BY BONE, AFTER SIR THOS. LAWRENCE.

Belonged to the Marquis Conyngham, after whose death it was given to the present Earl of Bradford by Lady Elizabeth Bryan.

29.

THE HON. MRS. PELHAM, DAUGHTER OF THE HON. BRIDGEMAN SIMPSON, AND WIFE OF CHARLES, AFTERWARDS FIRST EARL OF YARBOROUGH.

30.

VISCOUNT NEWPORT, AFTERWARDS SECOND EARL OF BRADFORD.

1818. BY ENGLEHART.

31.

GEORGINA ELIZABETH, VISCOUNTESS NEWPORT, WIFE OF THE ABOVE.

BY CHARLOTTE JONES.

Miniatures.

32.
SELINA LOUISA, VISCOUNTESS NEWPORT,
WIFE OF THE PRESENT AND THIRD EARL OF BRADFORD.

Full-length miniature.

BY THORBURN.

33.
HON. ISABELLA BYNG, AFTERWARDS MARCHIONESS OF BATH.

In a white satin case.

Given to the Countess of Bradford, on her marriage, by the Marquis of Bath.

34.
NAPOLEON BUONAPARTE.

A medallion.

35.
HON. LUCY BYNG, WIFE OF THE FIRST EARL OF BRADFORD.

Small miniature mounted on a red snuff-box.

36.
THE DUKE OF WELLINGTON.

A medallion.

37.
GEORGINA ELIZABETH, WIFE OF THE SECOND EARL OF BRADFORD.

AFTER SIR WILLIAM ROSS.

38.
GENERAL THE HON. JAMES RAMSAY.
By Miss G. E. Moncreiffe.

39.
MRS. HENRY TIGHE.
By Mrs. Kenyon.

40.
HON. LUCY BYNG, afterwards Wife of the First Earl of Bradford.

41.
SIR ORLANDO BRIDGEMAN, LORD-KEEPER.
From a portrait at Chirk Castle.
*By Miss Caroline Bridgeman Simpson.

LORD BRADFORD'S BEDROOM.

LORD BRADFORD'S BEDROOM.

TWO SKETCHES OF LORD ALBERT CONYNGHAM, AFTERWARDS FIRST LORD LONDESBOROUGH, WITH HIS SECOND WIFE.

HE WAS BORN 1805, DIED 1860.
SHE DIED 1883.

Two Sketches in Oils by Francis Grant, afterwards Sir Francis, P.R.A.

Design for a large Picture.

HE was the second surviving son of Henry, first Marquis Conyngham, by Elizabeth, daughter of Joseph Denison, Esq. of Denbies, County Surrey. Having succeeded to the large estates and fortunes of his maternal uncle, Lord Albert Conyngham assumed the surname and arms of Denison, and was elevated to the peerage by the title of Baron Londesborough. He married, first, in 1833, the Honourable Henrietta Maria Forester, fourth daughter of the first Baron Forester, who died in 1841. Lord Londesborough married, secondly, Ursula, daughter of Admiral the Honourable Charles Bridgeman, who became the wife of Lord Otho Fitzgerald.

THE THREE SONS OF GEORGE, VISCOUNT NEWPORT, PRESENT AND THIRD EARL OF BRADFORD.

With rocking-horse.

BY CALDERON, IN HIS VERY EARLY DAYS.

GEORGE C. O. BRIDGEMAN, present Viscount Newport. Born 1845; married, 1869, Lady Ida Lumley, daughter of the ninth Earl of Scarborough. Was in the Life Guards from 1864 till 1867. Was elected M.P. for the Northern Division of Shropshire from 1867 to 1885.

HONOURABLE FRANCIS BRIDGEMAN; born 1846; married, in 1883, Gertrude, daughter of George Hanbury, Esq. of Blythewood. Is in the Scots Guards, and M.P. for Bolton.

HONOURABLE GERALD BRIDGEMAN; born 1847; Lieutenant in Rifle Brigade. Died 1870.

LADIES SARAH AND CLEMENTINA VILLIERS.

BY CHALON.

THE daughters of the fifth Earl of Jersey, by Lady Sarah Fane, daughter of the tenth Earl of Westmoreland. Lady Sarah married, in 1842, Prince Nicholas Esterhazy, and died in 1853. Lady Clementina died in 1858.

CHARLOTTE, LADY SUFFIELD.

In crayons.

DIED 1859.

BY SLATER.

SHE was the only daughter of Alan Hyde, second Lord Gardner. Married, in 1835, Edward Vernon, fourth Baron Suffield, by whom she had no children.

LADY MABEL BRIDGEMAN.

BY E. CLIFFORD.

THE eldest daughter of the third and present Earl of Bradford. Married in 1887 to Colonel Kenyon-Slaney, Grenadier Guards, M.P. for Newport Division of Shropshire.

HON. G. C. O. BRIDGEMAN, THE PRESENT VISCOUNT NEWPORT (1888).

BORN 1845.

LADY BRADFORD'S ANTEROOM AND SITTING-ROOM.

LADY BRADFORD'S ANTEROOM.

LADY ALBERT CONYNGHAM.

DIED IN 1841.

By FRANCIS GRANT.

THE Hon. Henrietta Forester, married to Lord Albert Conyngham, afterwards Lord Londesborough, as his first wife.

QUEEN VICTORIA INVESTING THE SULTAN WITH THE ORDER OF THE GARTER ON BOARD THE ROYAL YACHT.

By G. THOMAS.

THIS picture was painted by permission of the Queen for Lord Bradford, who as Lord Chamberlain assisted at the ceremony. Mr. Thomas painted the same subject in a large picture for the Queen, and he died before he had finished this replica.

The Queen wished to confer the Order of the Garter upon the Sultan without any previous notice, and the Lord

Chamberlain was commissioned to borrow the Insignia from two of the Princes, K.G.s, who were on board. This he did by procuring the Blue Ribbon and George from Prince Arthur, and the Star from Prince Louis of Hesse. After the investiture the Sultan was told, through his interpreter, that the Queen had ordered more costly Insignia on purpose for His Imperial Majesty, and that as soon as these were ready they should be exchanged for those employed to-day. Upon which, without a moment's hesitation, the Sultan said to the Lord Chamberlain, through his interpreter, 'No, no, those which the Queen has herself placed on me, I will never part from.'

We are tempted to insert this anecdote as it has an historical interest, and one cannot but feel that the Sultan's speech betokened the chivalry of a newly dubbed knight.

JOHN GEORGE, LORD FORESTER.

Black Coat.

By ROTHWELL.

LADY BRADFORD'S SITTING-ROOM.

MARY ISABELLA, DUCHESS OF RUTLAND.

Small sketch in colours.

DIED 1831.

BY COSWAY.

SHE was the daughter of the fourth Duke of Beaufort, and married, in 1775, Charles, fourth Duke of Rutland. She was remarkable for her extreme beauty.

QUEEN VICTORIA IN ST. GEORGE'S CHAPEL AT THE MARRIAGE OF THE PRINCE OF WALES.

BY THOMAS.

THE HON. MABEL AND HON. FLORENCE BRIDGEMAN.

By A. Blakely.

DAUGHTERS of Viscount Newport, present and third Earl of Bradford.

HON. GERALD O. M. BRIDGEMAN.

BORN 1847, DIED 1870.

By Lundgren.

COUNTESS OF CHESTERFIELD.

DIED 1885.

By Miss Cruickshank, after Sir Edwin Landseer.

SHE was the eldest daughter of the first Lord Forester, consequently sister to the present Countess of Bradford. She married, in 1830, George Stanhope, sixth Earl of Chesterfield.

VESTIBULE.

VESTIBULE.

No. 1.   **COUNTESS OF BRADFORD.**

*White satin gown and lace.   Yellow rose.   Lace tie with jewel.
Lace head-dress.*

BY CLIFFORD.

SELINA LOUISA FORESTER, wife of Orlando G. C. Bridgeman, third Earl of Bradford.

No. 2.   **PORTRAIT. UNKNOWN.**

BY SIR PETER LELY.

No. 3.   **DIANA BRIDGEMAN.**

Blue low dress.   Lace stomacher and sleeves.   String of pearls.   Black cap.   White feather.

DIED 1764.

BY F. COTES.

SHE was the second daughter of Sir Orlando Bridgeman by Lady Anne Newport. She married John Sawbridge, Esq. of Ollantigh, County Kent.

No. 4.   LADY MYDDLETON.

Blue dress. White bodice. Large sleeves.

BY SIR GODFREY KNELLER.

HE was the only daughter of Sir Orlando Bridgeman, Lord Chief-Justice, and married Sir Thomas Myddleton, second Bart. of Chirk, as his second wife. Her only daughter Charlotte, married, first, Edward, Earl of Warwick, and secondly, the Right Hon. Joseph Addison, the celebrated author.

No. 5.   PORTRAIT. UNKNOWN.

BY SIR PETER LELY.

No. 6.   LADY MARY NEWPORT.

Blue dress. Short hair. King Charles's spaniel.

No. 7.

ELIZABETH, WIFE OF HENRY BRIDGEMAN, FIRST BARON BRADFORD.

BY PINE.

No. 10.   MARY QUEEN OF SCOTS.

AFTER ZUCCHERO.

Vestibule.

No. 11.   MISTRESS MARY, OR MOLL DAVIES.

Golden brown satin gown.

By Sir Peter Lely.

N the reign of Charles the Second, she was a member of the Duke of York's troop of comedians, and one of the four female actresses who boarded at Sir William Davenant's house. She was on the stage as early as 1664, in which year she appeared in 'The Stepmother,' and afterwards as Celia in 'The Rivals,' an adaptation by Davenant of the 'Two Noble Kinsmen.' Pepys makes frequent mention of her, and was a great admirer of her talent. He even pits her against Nell Gwynne: 'Little Mistress Davies danced a jig at the end of the play in boy's clothes, far superior to Nelly's performance in the same character.' It is true he calls her an impertinent slut, but that did not prevent the King from losing his heart, and my lady Castlemaine from being very jealous, seeing Charles's eyes were fixed all the time of the play on Mistress Moll. But what especially fascinated his Merry Majesty were the wild, mad, melodious songs she sang, and her wonderful grace and arch demeanour in dancing. Charles bought and furnished a house for her, and made her a present of a ring which cost £600, a large sum in those days. He had a daughter by her, called Mary Tudor, who was born in 1673, and married a son of Sir Francis Ratcliffe, afterwards Earl of Derwentwater.

No. 13.   PORTRAIT. UNKNOWN.

By Sir Antonio More.

PASSAGE—FIRST FLOOR.

PASSAGE—FIRST FLOOR.

SOUTH WALL.

No. 2.   MALE PORTRAIT. UNKNOWN.

Round black velvet hat. Long hair. Black velvet coat. Brown vest cut square. Chain and medallion. His right hand on baluster, holding a paper roll.

By PHILIP DE KONING.

No. 4.

ORLANDO BRIDGEMAN, ESQ., AFTERWARDS SECOND BARON AND FIRST EARL OF BRADFORD, 1815.

BORN 1762, DIED 1825.

As a youth. Light-coloured dress. White under sleeves. Lace collar with tassels. Long hair. Cloak, same colour as dress, over right shoulder.

No. 5.

GEORGE BYNG, FOURTH VISCOUNT TORRINGTON.

As a boy. Buff coat. White collar.

DIED 1812.

By RAMSAY.

THE eldest son of the third Viscount by Miss Daniel. He married in 1765 the Lady Lucy Boyle, the only daughter of John, Earl of Cork and Orrery, by whom he had four daughters, the eldest being the Countess of Bradford.

No. 6.

SECOND SIR ORLANDO BRIDGEMAN, FOURTH BARONET.

Claret coat. Powder.

BY F. COTES.

NELL GWYNNE.

Oval. Purple and white dress. Green and red bow on left shoulder. Pearl necklet.

DIED 1687.

BY MRS. BEALE.

SHE first attracted notice by her beauty and arch demeanour when selling oranges in the taverns and theatres. She studied acting under the elocutionists Hart and Lacy, both very much esteemed in the dramatic profession at the time. Her talents soon made her distinguished on the stage, but she seldom attempted tragedy. Her sprightliness and grace soon attracted the attention of the King, and before this period she was said to have counted the Duke of Buckingham and Lord Dorset among her admirers. The enemies of the Duchess of Cleveland were glad of an opportunity of recommending pretty Mistress Nell as a rival to the haughty beauty, to whom she stood in strange contrast, both in appearance and good-humour. In 1663 she was still a member of the King's company at Drury Lane, and was supposed to have quitted the stage about 1672. Pepys, in speaking of her in 1665, calls her 'pretty witty Nell,' and in 1666 he mentions that he went with his wife to see 'The Maiden Queen' by Dryden, in which there is a comical part taken by Nell that 'I never can hope to see the like done again by man or woman.' Also in the character of a mad girl and a young gallant, both admirable. But when she attempted such a part as the Emperor's daughter, good Samuel confesses she does it 'most basely.' Burnet designates her as the 'indiscreetest and wildest creature that ever was in a court.' Charles gave her a house in Pall Mall, in which we are told there was one room on the ground-floor of which the walls and ceiling were entirely composed of looking-glass. An anecdote is given of her, that, on one occasion when driving in a superb coach up Ludgate Hill, she met some bailiffs hurrying a clergyman to prison for debt. Inquiring as to the sum, she paid it on the spot, and later on procured preferment for him. Her son, afterwards Duke of St. Albans, was born in 1670 before she left the stage.

Dryden was a great admirer of pretty Nell, and wrote a prologue for her, which she spoke under a hat of such enormous dimensions as almost to conceal her small figure. The audience were convulsed with laughter, and Charles was almost suffocated.

Nell called his Majesty *her* Charles the Third, as she had had two protectors before who were his namesakes. Although thoughtless and reckless, she was a good friend to Charles in some respects, urging him constantly to pay more attention to public affairs, and interceding with him for objects of charity; she took a great interest in the foundation of Chelsea Hospital, and persuaded the King to hasten its completion. 'How am I to please my people?' he asked of her one day. 'There is but one way,' she replied: 'dismiss your ladies and attend to your business:' neither of which injunctions was obeyed. Nell Gwynne died at her house in Pall Mall in 1691, having survived the King some years, who, it will be remembered, in his last moments recommended her to the care of those who stood beside his bed. Dr. Tenison, afterwards Archbishop of Canterbury, preached her funeral sermon at the church of St. Martin's in the Fields, where she lies buried. There is little doubt she died a penitent.

No. 9.   PORTRAIT OF A LADY. UNKNOWN.

BY G. MORPHY.

WEST WALL.

No. 14.   PORTRAIT OF A LADY.

Low brown dress. White sleeves. Pearls in her hair. Little dog in her lap.

BY GREENHILL.

THIS lady is supposed to be Ursula, wife of Sir John Bridgeman.

No. 18.

FRANCIS NEWPORT, AFTERWARDS EARL OF BRADFORD.

Brown dress. Long hair. Lace cravat.

BY SIR GODFREY KNELLER.

No. 19.   GEORGE FORESTER, ESQUIRE.

Hunting dress. Fox's brush upon table.

BORN 1762, DIED 1811.

E was the son of Brook Forester, Esquire, by Elizabeth, daughter and heir of George Weld, Esquire of Willey Park, County Salop. George Forester never married, but left his fortune and estates to his cousin, Cecil Weld Forester, who was raised to the peerage as Baron Forester.

No. 20.

PORTRAIT OF A GENTLEMAN. UNKNOWN.

Red dress. Lace cravat. Short white wig.

No. 21.

JOHN BRIDGEMAN, BISHOP OF CHESTER.

Surplice and college cap. Arms of the See of Chester impaling Bridgeman in a shield above.

BORN 1577, DIED 1652.

BY VAN SOMERS.

No. 22.   COLONEL KINNEAR.

Blue coat. Powder.

DIED 1780.

BY F. COTES.

HE was Colonel of the 50th Regiment of Foot.

INDEX OF PORTRAITS.

INDEX OF PORTRAITS.

The Page marked in black figures gives the Biographical Notice.

	PAGE
ARUNDEL AND SURREY, EARL OF,	**124**
BATH, HON. ISABELLA BYNG, MARCHIONESS OF,	227
BAVARIA, PRINCESS OF (MARIA CHRISTINA),	214
BEDFORD, FRANCIS RUSSELL, FOURTH EARL OF,	**44**
... WILLIAM, FIRST DUKE OF,	**66**
BOLEYN, QUEEN ANN,	108
BRADFORD, LADY ELIZABETH,	207, 222, 244
FRANCIS NEWPORT, FIRST EARL OF,	**183**, 197, 253

Index of Portraits.

		PAGE
BRADFORD, GEORGE AUGUSTUS F. H. BRIDGEMAN, SECOND EARL OF,		202, 226
... GEORGINA MONCREIFFE, WIFE OF SECOND EARL OF,		225, 226, 227
... THE TWO ELDEST CHILDREN OF THE SECOND EARL,		226
... HENRY NEWPORT, THIRD EARL OF,		178
HENRY BRIDGEMAN, FIRST LORD,		208
... ... AND FAMILY,		117, 188
... LUCY BYNG, DOWAGER COUNTESS OF,		208, 221, 222, 223, 225, 227, 228
MARY, COUNTESS OF,		168
ORLANDO BRIDGEMAN, FIRST EARL OF,		109, 213, 224, 249
ORLANDO GEORGE CHARLES BRIDGEMAN, THIRD EARL OF,		119, 204, 216, 223, 226
THE THREE SONS OF THE THIRD EARL,		232
RICHARD NEWPORT, SECOND EARL OF,		169
SELINA LOUISA, COUNTESS OF,		103, 216, 227, 243
BRIDGEMAN, LADY ANNE,		180
CHARLES, THE HONOURABLE CAPTAIN, R.N.,		102
CHARLOTTE,		190

Index of Portraits.

		PAGE
BRIDGEMAN, DIANA,		243
	ELIZABETH, WIFE OF BISHOP JOHN,	189
...	ELIZABETH, HONOURABLE,	189, 222
	FRANCIS, HONOURABLE,	232
...	GEORGE, ESQUIRE,	117
	GEORGE, HONOURABLE AND REVEREND,	111, 225
	GERALD, THE HONOURABLE,	232, 240
	HENRY, THE HONOURABLE,	212
	JOHN, BISHOP OF CHESTER,	175, 254
	SIR JOHN, SECOND BARONET,	182
	... THIRD BARONET,	187
	LUCY, LADY,	224
	MABEL, LADY,	233
	LADIES MABEL AND FLORENCE,	240
	SIR ORLANDO, LORD KEEPER,	18, 170, 228
	ORLANDO, ESQUIRE,	190
	AFTERWARDS FIRST EARL OF BRADFORD,	109, 213, 224, 249
	THE HON. AND WIFE, AFTERWARDS FIRST EARL AND COUNTESS,	223
	... FOURTH BARONET,	177, 250
...	... THE HONOURABLE, GRENADIER GUARDS,	101

Index of Portraits.

PAGE

BRIDGEMAN, ORLANDO G. C., THE HON., AS A CHILD, AFTERWARDS THIRD EARL OF BRADFORD, . . 119
THE THREE SONS OF THE THIRD EARL OF BRADFORD, . . 232
URSULA, WIFE OF SIR JOHN, THIRD BARONET, (Qu.), . 252
BUONAPARTE, NAPOLEON, EMPEROR OF FRANCE, ... 107, 227
BYNG, HONOURABLE LUCY, 208, 221, 222, 223, 225, 227, 228
... GEORGE, . . 223
HONOURABLE GEORGIANA, 225

CAREW, SIR NICHOLAS, . . 138
CARLISLE, COUNTESS OF, AND NIECE, . 123
CHARLES THE FIRST, KING, . . 130
CHAPPELOW, REVEREND LEONARD, . 213
... ... WHEN A YOUTH, . 224
CHESTER, JOHN BRIDGEMAN, BISHOP OF CHESTER, . . 175, 254
... ELIZABETH, WIFE OF, 189
CHESTERFIELD, COUNTESS OF, 240
CONYNGHAM, LORD ALBERT, . . 231
LADY ALBERT, FIRST WIFE, . 237
... ... SECOND WIFE, 231
CORK AND ORRERY, JOHN BOYLE, FIFTH EARL OF, ... 224

Index of Portraits.

	PAGE
DALHOUSIE, MARQUESS OF,	203
DAVIES, MISTRESS MARY,	245
DERBY, EDWARD STANLEY, FOURTEENTH EARL OF,	110
DIGBY, SIR KENELM,	141
DORMER, LADY ISABELLA,	95
DYSART, LIONEL TOLLEMACHE, SECOND EARL OF,	191
COUNTESS OF,	167
ESSEX, THOMAS CROMWELL, EARL OF,	155
FEILDING, LADY DIANA,	96
FORESTER, GEORGE, ESQUIRE,	253
LORD,	238
GEORGE THE SECOND, KING OF ENGLAND,	109
... THE FOURTH,	226
GERMANY, WILLIAM THE FIRST, EMPEROR OF,	224
GORING, COLONEL, AFTERWARDS LORD,	80
GROTIUS, HUGO,	19
GUNNING, HON. MRS.,	189, 222
... SIR GEORGE,	114
GWYNNE, NELL,	250
HAMET BEN HAMET,	208
HARVEY, DR.,	57

2 L

Index of Portraits.

	PAGE
HERBERT, HENRY, FOURTH LORD OF RIPSFORD,	181
... MISTRESS, ...	153
HOLLAND, HENRY RICH, FIRST EARL OF,	195
JOSEPHINE, EMPRESS OF FRANCE,	222
KILLIGREW, SIR THOMAS, .	148
... LADY, .	163
KINGSTON, COUNTESS OF, .	211
KINNEAR, COLONEL, .	254
LEWIS, HENRY GRESWOLD, ...	111
LIVERPOOL, ROBERT JENKINSON, SECOND EARL OF, ...	104
LOWTHER, SIR WILLIAM,	114
LYNEDOCH, LORD,	201
MAURICE, PRINCE, ...	75
MONCREIFFE, SIR THOMAS, AND SISTER,	209
GEORGINA, WIFE OF THE SECOND EARL OF BRADFORD, .	225, 226, 227
MORTIMER, CAPTAIN, . .	210
MYDDLETON, SIR THOMAS, .	71
LADY, . .	244
NEWPORT, ANDREW, THE HONOURABLE, .	36
... LADY MARY,	244

Index of Portraits.

	PAGE
NEWPORT, RICHARD, SECOND EARL OF BRADFORD,	169
... VISCOUNT, GEORGE A. BRIDGEMAN, AFTERWARDS SECOND EARL OF BRADFORD,	202, 226
VISCOUNTESS, HIS WIFE GEORGINA,	225, 226, 227
VISCOUNT, ORLANDO GEORGE CHARLES BRIDGEMAN, AFTERWARDS THIRD EARL OF BRADFORD,	119, 204, 216, 223, 226
THE THIRD EARL AND HIS WIFE,	216
THE THREE SONS OF THE THIRD EARL,	232
VISCOUNT, SON OF THIRD EARL OF BRADFORD,	232, 233
OXFORD, COUNTESS OF,	141
PAYNE, CAPTAIN JOHN WILLETT,	118
PELHAM, THE HONOURABLE MRS.,	226
PORTRAITS UNKNOWN, ETC.,	97, 104, 130, 133, 134, 138, 140, 141, 192, 201, 221, 243, 244, 245, 249, 252, 253.
QUEEN VICTORIA,	109, 210, 217
INVESTITURE OF THE SULTAN,	237
MARRIAGE OF THE PRINCE OF WALES,	239
RAMSAY, GENERAL THE HON. JAMES,	228

	AGE
RICHARD THE THIRD, KING (*Qu.*),	104
RUPERT, PRINCE,	83
RUSSELL, LADY DIANA, . . .	91, 123
... DIANA, LADY RUSSELL, YOUNGEST DAUGHTER OF THE THIRD EARL OF BEDFORD, . .	97
EDWARD, THE HONOURABLE,	65
FRANCIS, THE HONOURABLE, .	72
... JOHN, THE HONOURABLE, COLONEL,	43
LORD JOHN, .	211
LADY JOHN,	223, 225
LADY RACHEL, .	3
LORD ROBERT, .	18
LADY ROBERT,	17
... LORD WILLIAM, .	48
RUSSIA, ALEXANDER II., CZAR OF, .	222
RUTLAND, MARY ISABELLA, DUCHESS OF,	239
SALTREN, MRS., . .	222
SCOTS, MARY QUEEN OF,	207, 244
SCOTT, MRS., . . .	224
SEYMOUR, LORD HUGH, VICE-ADMIRAL,	115
SIMPSON, HONOURABLE JOHN BRIDGEMAN, .	113
... HONOURABLE MRS.,	209, 221
SOMERSET, EDWARD SEYMOUR, DUKE OF (PROTECTOR), .	131

Index of Portraits.

	PAGE
SOUTHAMPTON, THOMAS WRIOTHESLEY, EARL OF, . .	78
STRAFFORD, EARL OF, AND HIS SECRETARY,	37
SUFFIELD, CHARLOTTE, LADY, .	233
SUNDERLAND, DOROTHY, COUNTESS OF,	125
TIGHE, MRS. HENRY, ...	228
TORRINGTON, GEORGE BYNG, FOURTH VISCOUNT, .	225, 249
... VISCOUNTESS,	191
TURENNE, MARSHAL, . . .	197
TURKEY, SULTAN OF, INVESTITURE OF,	237

UNKNOWN PORTRAITS, ETC., 97, 104, 130, 133, 134, 138, 140, 141, 192, 201, 221, 224, 243, 244, 245, 249, 252, 253.

VANDERNERCK, .	225
VANDYCK, ANTHONY,	134
VILLIERS, LADIES SARAH AND CLEMENTINA,	232
WALES, PRINCE OF, MARRIAGE OF,	239
WELLINGTON, DUKE OF, .	204, 210, 227
WEST, COLONEL,	78
WHITMORE, LADY LUCY,	225

Index of Portraits.

	PAGE
WILBRAHAM, SIR THOMAS,	186
... LADY,	186
WORSLEY, MISS,	209, 221
YATES, MARY,	207

ERRATA.

Page 43, line 6, *for* youngest *read* third.
,, 57, line 14, after Riley put (?).
,, 71, last line, *for* Woodney *read* Woodhey.
,, 103, line 3, *for* Elizabeth Anne, *read* Eliza Caroline.
,, 117, line 4, *dele* (?).
,, 170, line 5, *for* Riley *read* Sir Peter Lely.
,, 175, line 6, *for* Born 1575, Died 1657-8.
read Born 1577, Died 1652.
,, 208, line 4, *for* only *read* eldest surviving.
,, 210, line 6, *dele* the words 'for the Earl of Bradford.'
,, 222, line 7 from foot, *for* Salken *read* Saltren.
,, 223, line 11, *for* '*née* Seymour' *read* '*née* Davies, niece of Mr. Seymour.'
,, 226, line 2, *for* two *read* five.

www.ingramcontent.com/pod-product-compliance
Lightning Source LLC
Chambersburg PA
CBHW031938230426
43672CB00010B/1960